AMERICAN JOURNAL

AMERICAN JOURNAL

FIFTY POEMS FOR OUR TIME

SELECTED AND WITH AN INTRODUCTION BY

TRACY K. SMITH

GRAYWOLF PRESS
IN ASSOCIATION WITH THE LIBRARY OF CONGRESS

Permission acknowledgments appear on pages 115–120.

This publication is made possible, in part, by the voters of Minnesota through a Minnesota State Arts Board Operating Support grant, thanks to a legislative appropriation from the arts and cultural heritage fund, and a grant from the Wells Fargo Foundation. Significant support has also been provided by Target, the McKnight Foundation, the Lannan Foundation, the Amazon Literary Partnership, and other generous contributions from foundations, corporations, and individuals. To these organizations and individuals we offer our heartfelt thanks.

Published by Graywolf Press, in association with the Library of Congress
250 Third Avenue North, Suite 600
Minneapolis, Minnesota 55401

www.graywolfpress.org

Published in the United States of America

ISBN 978-1-55597-838-9 (cloth)
ISBN 978-1-55597-815-0 (paper)

6 8 10 12 11 9 7 5

Library of Congress Control Number: 2018934515 (cloth), 2018934515 (paper)

Cover design: Kyle G. Hunter

Cover art: Upper left: *In 1993, Thomas Crawford's Statue of Freedom was removed by helicopter from the U.S. Capitol dome for restoration. Washington, D.C.*, by Carol Highsmith, 1993. Carol M. Highsmith Archive, Library of Congress, Prints and Photographs Division, LC-DIG-highsm-13969. Upper right: *Maria Gomez, 3466 2nd Ave., LA*, by Camilo José Vergara, 2003. Library of Congress, Prints & Photographs Division, LC-DIG-vrg-00309. Lower left: *Richard Ortiz is a migrant worker in Nipomo, California, where famous photographer Dorothea Lange took a photograph of the Migrant Mother, Florence Owens Thompson in the 1930s*, by Carol Highsmith, 2013. The Jon B. Lovelace Collection of California Photographs in Carol M. Highsmith's America Project, Library of Congress, Prints and Photographs Division, LC-DIG-highsm-25212. Lower right (top): *"Sno-cone" stand, New Orleans, Louisiana*, by Carol Highsmith, between 1980 and 2006. Carol M. Highsmith Archive, Library of Congress, Prints and Photographs Division, LC-DIG-highsm-13991. Lower right (bottom): *Aerial view of mountaintop removal, approaching Racine*, by Lyntha Scott Eiler, 1995. Coal River Folklife Collection (AFC 1999/008), Library of Congress, American Folklife Center.

CONTENTS

AMERICAN JOURNAL

This is why I love poems: they invite me to sit down and listen to a voice speaking thoughtfully and passionately about what it feels like to be alive. Usually the someone doing the talking—the poem's speaker—is a person I'd never get the chance to meet were it not for the poem. Because the distance between us is too great. Or because we are too unlike one another to ever feel this at ease face-to-face. Or maybe because the person talking to me never actually existed as anything other than a figment of a poet's imagination, a character invented for reasons I may not ever know. Even when that someone is the real-life poet speaking of things that have actually happened, there is something different—some new strength, vulnerability, or authority—that the poem fosters. This is why I love poems: they require me to sit still, listen deeply, and imagine putting myself in someone else's unfamiliar shoes. The world I return to when the poem is over seems fuller and more comprehensible as a result.

American Journal: Fifty Poems for Our Time is an offering for people who love poems the way I do. It is also an offering for those who love them in different ways, and those who don't yet know what their relationship with poetry will be. I hope there is even something here to please readers who, for whatever the reason, might feel themselves to be at odds with poetry. These fifty poems—culled from living American poets of different ages, backgrounds, and aesthetic approaches, and with different views of what it feels like to be alive—welcome you to listen and be surprised, amused, consoled. These poems invite you to remember something you once knew, to see something you've never seen, and to range from one set of concerns to another. For the time that you are reading them, and even after, these poems will collapse the distance between you and fifty different real or imagined people with fifty different outlooks on the human condition.

But how? How do poems capture the significant yet hard-to-describe events and feelings punctuating our lives, and our time?

Poems call upon sounds and silence to operate like music. They invoke vivid sensory images to make abstract feelings like love or anger or doubt feel solid and unmistakable. Like movies, poems slow time down or speed it up; they cross cut from one viewpoint to another as a way of discerning connections between unlikely things; they use line and stanza breaks to create suspense. Even the visual layout of words on the page is a device to help conduct a reader's movement through the encounter that is the poem. These and other tools help poems call our attention to moments when the ordinary nature of experience changes—when the things we think we know flare into brighter colors, starker contrasts, strange and intoxicating possibilities.

There's something else these fifty poems are up to. As the title *American Journal* suggests, they are contemplating what it feels like to live, work, love, strive, raise a family, and survive many kinds of loss in this vast and varied nation. The great poet Robert Hayden, from Detroit, Michigan, was the first African American to serve in the role now known as Poet Laureate of the United States. His final collection contains an extraordinary poem called "[American Journal]," which is written in the voice of an alien from outer space sent to earth to observe humankind. On this planet, the speaker finds himself most drawn to "the americans," whom he calls "this baffling multi people." He recognizes America as a land of contrasts and contradictions, a place still new, still reckoning with the implications of its history. While much of life in this nation strikes him as strange, some of what he observes people doing reaches him as familiar:

> like us they have created a veritable populace
> of machines that serve and soothe and pamper
> and entertain   we have seen their flags and
> foot prints on the moon   also the intricate
> rubbish left behind   a wastefully ingenious
> people   many it appears worship the Unknowable
> Essence   the same for them as for us

And some of it, he finds perplexing:

> america   as much a problem in metaphysics as
> it is a nation earthly entity an iota in our
> galaxy   an organism that changes even as i
> examine it   fact and fantasy never twice the
> same   so many variables

Like many poets, Hayden allows his poem's speaker to build upon what may be the poet's own complicated relationship to his subject matter. This figure from another planet, who moves through human society without ever being fully integrated into it or understood by his peers, provides the poet with the occasion and the means to explore the real-life experience of social alienation, of being a part of—and yet also at times apart from—a larger group.

I'm drawn to Hayden's poem because it paints a loving yet critical portrait of a nation in progress, and because it emphasizes the many forms that Americanness takes. In borrowing its title, I'm hoping to make space for new reports on the American experience in our time.

These fifty poems take up stories old and new, and traditions deeply rooted and newly arrived. They bear witness to the daily struggles and promises of community, as well as to the times when community eludes us. They celebrate us and the natural world, and bow in reverence to the mysterious unknown. They do this and, inevitably, a great deal more. I am also hoping that their courage, intimacy of address, and even the journey they collectively map out—a journey that encompasses consideration of place; reflections on family and individual identity; responses to the urgencies affecting our collective culture; and gestures of love, hope, and remembrance—might go some way toward making us, whoever and wherever we are, a little less alien to one another.

Tracy K. Smith
Princeton, New Jersey

I. THE SMALL TOWN OF MY YOUTH

Second Estrangement

Please raise your hand,
whomever else of you
has been a child,
lost, in a market
or a mall, without
knowing it at first, following
a stranger, accidentally
thinking he is yours,
your family or parent, even
grabbing for his hands,
even calling the word
you said then for "Father,"
only to see the face
look strangely down, utterly
foreign, utterly not the one
who loves you, you
who are a bird suddenly
stunned by the glass partitions
of rooms.
          How far
the world you knew, & tall,
& filled, finally, with strangers.

In Defense of Small Towns

When I look at it, it's simple, really. I hated life there. September,
once filled with animal deaths and toughened hay. And the smells

of fall were boiled-down beets and potatoes
or the farmhands' breeches smeared with oil and diesel

as they rode into town, dusty and pissed. The radio station
split time between metal and Tejano, and the only action

happened on Friday nights where the high school football team
gave everyone a chance at forgiveness. The town left no room

for novelty or change. The sheriff knew everyone's son and
     despite that,
we'd cruise up and down the avenues, switching between

brake and gearshift. We'd fight and spit chew into Big Gulp cups
and have our hearts broken nightly. In that town I learned

to fire a shotgun at nine and wring a chicken's neck
with one hand by twirling the bird and whipping it straight like
     a towel.

But I loved the place once. Everything was blonde and cracked
and the irrigation ditches stretched to the end of the earth.
     You could

ride on a bicycle and see clearly the outline of every leaf
or catch on the streets each word of a neighbor's argument.

Nothing could happen there and if I willed it, the place would
    have me
slipping over its rocks into the river with the sugar plant's steam

or signing papers at a storefront army desk, buttoned up
with medallions and a crew cut, eyeing the next recruits.

If I've learned anything, it's that I could be anywhere,
staring at a hunk of asphalt or listening to the clap of billiard balls

against each other in a bar and hear my name. Indifference now?
Some. I shook loose, but that isn't the whole story. The fact is

I'm still in love. And when I wake up, I watch my son yawn,
and my mind turns his upswept hair into cornstalks

at the edge of a field. Stillness is an acre, and his body
idles, deep like heavy machinery. I want to take him back there,

to the small town of my youth and hold the book of wildflowers
open for him, and look. I want him to know the colors of horses,

to run with a cattail in his hand and watch as its seeds
fly weightless as though nothing mattered, as though

the little things we tell ourselves about our pasts stay there,
rising slightly and just out of reach.

'N'em

They said to say goodnight
And not goodbye, unplugged
The TV when it rained. They hid
Money in mattresses
So to sleep on decisions.
Some of their children
Were not their children. Some
Of their parents had no birthdates.
They could sweat a cold out
Of you. They'd wake without
An alarm telling them to.
Even the short ones reached
Certain shelves. Even the skinny
Cooked animals too quick
To catch. And I don't care
How ugly one of them arrived,
That one got married
To somebody fine. They fed
Families with change and wiped
Their kitchens clean.
Then another century came.
People like me forgot their names.

Flat as a Flitter

The way you can crush a bug
or stomp drained cans of Schlitz out on the porch,

the bread when it won't rise,
the cake when it falls after the oven-door slams—

the old people had their way
to describe such things. "But what's a flitter?"

I always asked my granny. And she could never say.
"It's just a flitter. Well, it might be a fritter."

"Then why not say 'fritter'?"
"Shit, Melissa. Because the old people said 'flitter.'"

And she smacked the fried pie into the skillet,
and banged the skillet on the stove,

and shook and turned the pie
till it was on its way to burnt.

Flatter than a flitter, a mountain
when its top's blown off:

dynamited, shaved to the seam,
the spoil pushed into hollers, into streams,

the arsenic slurry caged behind a dam,
teetering above an elementary school.

The old people said "flitter." They didn't live to see
God's own mountain turned

hazard-orange mid-air pond,
a haze of waste whose brightness rivals heaven.

When that I was a little bitty baby,
my daddy drove up into Virginia

to fix strip-mining equipment, everything
to him an innocent machine in need.

On God's own mountain,
poor people drink bad water, and the heart

of the Lord is a seam of coal gouged out
to fuel the light in other places.

The old people didn't live
to give a name to this

kingdom of gravel and blast.
Lay me a hunk of coal

on my flittered tongue
to mark the mountains' graves,

to mark my father's tools
quarrying bread for my baby plate,

to mark my granny slapping dough
as if with God's own flat hand.

Sugar and Brine: Ella's Understanding

Daddy slaughtered the hog right there in the side yard,
and it hurt to see it, but that won't stop me from eating.
Come Thanksgiving, I'll dip a bit of ham in Jackson's
Ribbon Cane Syrup, and pop it inside a biscuit.
When it's time to celebrate, something dies.
When something dies, we take it with the sweet.

Take my cousin Gerald—he left us last summer,
a tractor accident. We were cousins by marriage, but
friends by choice, so I cried more than when I broke my leg
jumping off the front porch—bone snapped clean through.
After the funeral, as the Lord is my witness,
those were the best potato pies I ever had.

Yesterday, where the yellow pines meet the creek,
that boy on the other side of the property line
helped bring his daddy's cattle in. I watched him watch
me standing in a field littered with cow's corn,
my head tilted just enough to let him know I was
curious. He left a scarlet ribbon tied to the barbed wire.
My heart skipped quicker than a swallow's when I found it.
Now I'm wondering what throat's going to open?
I need to warn him—the wheel never rusts, never stops.

The Field Trip

This time they're thirteen, no longer
interested in the trillium on the path but in each other,
though they will not say so. Only the chaperone
lingers at the adder's-tongue,
watching the teacher trail the rest uphill
to where the dense virginal forest thins and opens.
At the clearing, she tells them to be still and mute
and make a list of what they see and hear.
A girl asks if she should also list
the way she feels—she's the one
who'll cite the shadow on the lake below.
The others sprawl on gender-separate rocks
except for the smart-ass, perched
on the cliff-edge, inviting front-page photos—
PICNIC MARRED BY TRAGEDY. From time to time,
in the midst of the day's continual lunch,
as the students read the lists their teacher edits,
the boy swears and stretches—
he is in fact fourteen, doing seventh grade
a second time, this same assignment
also a second time. Pressed, he says
he sees exactly what he saw before—ponds, rocks, trees—
shouting it back from the same vantage point
out on the twelve-inch ledge,
Long Pond a ragged puddle underneath him;
and what he shouts grows more and more
dangerously insubordinate as he leans

more and more dramatically over the edge.
But he is, after all, the first to spot the hawk;
and it is, looking down on it, amazing. The others
gather near the unimpeded view,
together, finally, standing on this bluff
overlooking three natural ponds, hearing the wind
ruffle the cedar fringe, watching the hawk
float along the thermals like a leaf.
And for a moment, belittled by indifferent wilderness,
you want to praise the boy, so much does he resemble
if not the hawk then the doomed shrub
fanned against the rockface there beside him,
rooted in a fissure in the rock.
But soon the hero swings back up to earth,
the group divides. Just like that
they're ready for home, tired of practicing:
sixteen children, two adults, and one
bad boy who carved a scorpion on his arm.

Mighty Pawns

If I told you Earl, the toughest kid
on my block in North Philadelphia,
bow-legged and ominous, could beat
any man or woman in ten moves playing white,
or that he traveled to Yugoslavia to frustrate the bearded
masters at the Belgrade Chess Association,
you'd think I was given to hyperbole,
and if, at dinnertime, I took you
into the faint light of his Section 8 home
reeking of onions, liver, and gravy,
his six little brothers fighting on a broken love-seat
for room in front of a cracked flat-screen,
one whose diaper sags it's a wonder
it hasn't fallen to his ankles,
the walls behind doors exposing sheetrock
the perfect O of a handle, and the slats
of stairs missing where Baby-boy gets stuck
trying to ascend to a dominion foreign to you and me
with its loud timbales and drums blasting down
from the closed room of his cousin whose mother
stands on a corner on the other side of town
all times of day and night, except when her relief
check arrives at the beginning of the month,
you'd get a better picture of Earl's ferocity
after-school on the board in Mr. Sherman's class,
but not necessarily when he stands near you
at a downtown bus-stop in a jacket a size too

small, hunching his shoulders around his ears,
as you imagine the checkered squares of his poverty
and anger, and pray he does not turn his precise gaze
too long in your direction for fear he blames
you and proceeds to take your Queen.

FROM *summer, somewhere*

somewhere, a sun. below, boys brown
as rye play the dozens & ball, jump

in the air & stay there. boys become new
moons, gum-dark on all sides, beg bruise

-blue water to fly, at least tide, at least
spit back a father or two. i won't get started.

history is what it is. it knows what it did.
bad dog. bad blood. bad day to be a boy

color of a July well spent. but here, not earth
not heaven, we can't recall our white shirts

turned ruby gowns. here, there's no language
for *officer* or *law*, no color to call *white*.

if snow fell, it'd fall black. please, don't call
us dead, call us alive someplace better.

we say our own names when we pray.
we go out for sweets & come back.

Walking Home

Everything dies, I said. How had that started?

A tree? The winter? Not me, she said.

And I said, Oh yeah? And she said, I'm reincarnating.

Ha, she said, See you in a few thousand years!

Why years, I wondered, why not minutes? Days?

She found that so funny—Ha Ha—doubled over—

Years, she said, confidently.

I think you and I have known each other a few lifetimes, I said.

She said, I have never before been a soul on this earth.

(It was cold. We were hungry.) Next time, you be the mother,
     I said.

No way, Jose, she said, as we turned the last windy corner.

Music from Childhood

You grow up hearing two languages. Neither fits your fits
Your mother informs you "moon" means "window to another
world."

You begin to hear words mourn the sounds buried inside their
mouths
A row of yellow windows and a painting of them

Your mother informs you "moon" means "window to another
world."
You decide it is better to step back and sit in the shadows

A row of yellow windows and a painting of them
Someone said you can see a blue pagoda or a red rocket ship

You decide it is better to step back and sit in the shadows
Is it because you saw a black asteroid fly past your window

Someone said you can see a blue pagoda or a red rocket ship
I tried to follow in your footsteps, but they turned to water

Is it because I saw a black asteroid fly past my window
The air hums—a circus performer riding a bicycle towards the
ceiling

I tried to follow in your footsteps, but they turned to water
The town has started sinking back into its commercial

The air hums—a circus performer riding a bicycle towards the
    ceiling
You grow up hearing two languages. Neither fits your fits

The town has started sinking back into its commercial
You begin to hear words mourn the sounds buried inside their
    mouths

Girls Overheard While Assembling a Puzzle

Are you sure this blue is the same as the
blue over there? This wall's like the
bottom of a pool, its
color I mean. I need a
darker two-piece this summer, the kind with
elastic at the waist so it actually
fits. I can't
find her hands. Where does this gold
go? It's like the angel's giving
her a little piece of honeycomb to eat.
I don't see why God doesn't
just come down and
kiss her himself. This is the red of that
lipstick we saw at the
mall. This piece of her
neck could fit into the light part
of the sky. I think this is a
piece of water. What kind of
queen? You mean
right here? And are we supposed to believe
she can suddenly
talk angel? Who thought this stuff
up? I wish I had a
velvet bikini. That flower's the color of the
veins in my grandmother's hands. I
wish we could

walk into that garden and pick an
X-ray to float on.
Yeah. I do too. I'd say a
zillion yeses to anyone for that.

Passing

At a station in a no-name town,
a blue-red coleus

blooms from a cleft in the track.
Too obvious, I say, out loud

to the window, to God,
to no one, rolling my white eyes

into my thick bright head.
If I arrive,

who will greet me as brother,
as owner, who will greet me

at all, feeling from my veins
the pull of our one long pulse—

Pissing into the metal bin, my waste
streaming out onto the track,

I laugh at the mirror, an animal,
unhinging, trying

to see what they see
in whatever I am standing here—Then

the train slides into a long tunnel.
The lights flicker off

and I am back inside my mother.

II. SOMETHING SHINES OUT FROM EVERY DARKNESS

"Let me tell you about my marvelous god"

Let me tell you about my marvelous god, how he hides in the
    hexagons
of the bees, how the drought that wrings its leather hands
above the world is of his making, as well as the rain in the quiet
    minutes
that leave only thoughts of rain.
An atom is working and working, an atom is working in deepest
night, then bursting like the farthest star; it is far
smaller than a pinprick, far smaller than a zero and it has no
will, no will toward us.
This is why the heart has paced and paced,
will pace and pace across the field where yarrow
was and now is dust. A leaf catches
in a bone. The burrow's shut by a tumbled clod
and the roots, upturned, are hot to the touch.
How my god is a feathered and whirling thing; you will singe
    your arm
when you pluck him from the air,
when you pluck him from that sky
where sorrow swirls, and you will burn again
throwing him back.

Sister as Moving Object

my sister is moving in me again
with her long   arms and legs

moving to tell me   she's still here
inside my body   along with fireballs

free-roaming breath   some days she's a tanker truck
magnetic   gleaming down my highways

some days   an ocean liner   splitting
the dark waters   today   my sister's particular beauty

rocks the house   to 1965   wearing pink-pink-
caked-on lipstick   tight pants   teased-up-

Ann-Margaret hair   could've been anyone's
sister and was   adopted from another place

she raised me up   taught me   the necessary things:
how to mix   water with bourbon   in the picture-frame bar

how to mix   the real and the unreal   and make it glisten
sea of submerged heartache   great blanket of sea:

seamount   *sweptback*   *from the guyot to the springboard*
sluice   *railbed*   *heart of copper field*

nightshade   when she hid her arsonist boyfriend
in the basement closet   (when the cops came looking for him)

she taught me the power of a lie: *no, I haven't seen him*
no, not since yesterday   she taught me to be visible   then follow

the circle down: *ball bearings   axehandles*
fields of snakes   hot spur of escape   when she ran downstairs

to tip him off: *now! through the backyards*
they won't look there   she gave and gave   early lessons in desire

her and her dark-haired muscle boy   on the rock
behind the shopping center   me the lookout   air thick

with everything coming   his thin teeshirt   i watched their mouths:
|torrential| everything i wanted   moving through them

today I name the lasting roads: *artery   toll road   road of disguise*
she taught me imprisonment   not being a rat:

I took to the heat   like a dog to an electric fence   don't go past
the edge of the yard   2 girls blank from no beginnings   in combat

so tall   the only way to beat her   was to scissor her
between my thick legs   and squeeze

tonight   the house humming   her particular beauty:
lack of compromise   she grabbed the nail scissors   stabbed me:

sea of the head thrown back   she, later   dancing to loud music
said: *do it like this, don't listen*   *to what they tell you*

sea we never shared   blood sea

FROM *The Split*

1. She was starting to look like her mother.
2. She was clingier than pantyhose.
3. He stayed out all night.
4. She liked to cuff me when she got plowed.
5. He was vapid.
6. She was a fool.
7. She ridiculed me in front of the dogs.
8. He stuck a hairpin in my ear.
9. He had an affair with my older sister.
10. He spent our money on booze and bennies.
11. She wouldn't clean and it stank like bad beef.
12. I tried to hang myself but it didn't work.
13. He didn't like my sweet potato pie and said his mother made it better.
14. She wouldn't learn trigonometry for me.
15. I took it all out on the little ones.
16. She couldn't get pregnant.
17. He was shooting blanks.
18. He made for a pitiful sight in a bathing suit.
19. I wanted out, then I didn't, then I did.
20. I just couldn't live without Sally.
21. He wanted to start a family and to start it now, with me.
22. She split when the money ran out.
23. I gave her three more chances and then I left.
24. She hated the Dave Clark Five.
25. I was indentured. I didn't know I could choose not to.
26. He went out for gum etcetera.

27. By April she had passed on.
28. He saw only his idea of me.
29. We couldn't agree on an invitation font.
30. He was bad news, and it's always, like, *bad news, here I am.*

The Hypno-Domme Speaks, and Speaks and Speaks

I was born as a woman, I talk you to death,
$\qquad$ or else your ear off,
or else you to sleep. What do I have, all the time
in the world, and a voice that swings brass back
and forth, you can hear it, and a focal point where
my face should be. What do I have, I have absolute
power, and what I want is your money, your drool,
and your mind, and the sense of myself as a snake,
and a garter in the grass. Every bone in the snake
is the hipbone, every part of the snake is the hips.
The first sound I make is silence, then sssssshhh,
$\qquad$ the first word I say is listen. Sheep shearers
$\qquad$ and accountants hypnotize the hardest,
and lookout sailors who watch the sea, and the boys
who cut and cut and cut and cut and cut the grass.
The writers who write page-turners, and the writers
who repeat themselves. The diamond-cutter kneels
down before me and asks me to hypnotize him, and
I glisten at him and glisten hard, and listen to me and
listen, I tell him. Count your age backward, I tell him.
Become aware of your breathing, and aware of mine
$\qquad$ which will go on longer. Believe you
$\qquad$ are a baby till I tell you otherwise, then believe
you're a man till I tell you you're dirt. When a gunshot
rings out you'll lie down like you're dead. When you
$\qquad$ hear, "He is breathing," you'll stand up again.
The best dog of the language is Yes and protects you.

The best black-and-white dog of the language is Yes
and goes wherever you go, and you go where I say,
you go anywhere. Why do I do it is easy, I am working
my way through school. Give me the money
                    for Modernism, and give me the money
for what comes next. When you wake to the fact that you
have a body, you will wake to the fact that not for long.
When you wake you will come when you read the word
hard, or hard to understand me, or impenetrable poetry.
When you put down the book you will come when you
hear the words put down the book,
                    you will come when you hear.

The Poet at Fifteen
    after Larry Levis

You wear faded black
and paint your face white as the blessed
teeth of Jesus
because brown isn't high art
unless you are a beautiful savage.

All the useless tautologies—

This is me. I am this. I am me.

In your ragged
Salvation Army sweaters, in your brilliant

awkwardness. White dresses
like Emily Dickinson.

I dreaded that first Robin,
so, at fifteen you slash
your wrists.

You're not allowed
to shave your legs in the hospital.

The atmosphere
that year: sometimes you exist
and sometimes you think you're Mrs. Dalloway.

This is bold—existing.

You do not understand your parents
who understand you less:
your father who listens to ABBA after work,
your mother who eats expired food.

How do you explain what you have done?
With your hybrid mouth, a split tongue.

How do you explain the warmth
sucking you open, leaving you
like a gutted machine?

It is a luxury to tell a story.

How do you explain
that the words are made by more
than your wanting?

Te chingas o te jodes.

At times when you speak Spanish, your tongue
is flaccid inside your rotten mouth:

desgraciada, sin vergüenza.

At the hospital they're calling your name
with an accent on the *E*. They bring you
tacos, a tiny golden crucifix.

Your father has run
all the way from the factory.

My Brother at 3 AM

He sat cross-legged, weeping on the steps
when Mom unlocked and opened the front door.
    O God, he said, *O God.*
        He wants to kill me, Mom.

When Mom unlocked and opened the front door
at 3 a.m., she was in her nightgown, Dad was asleep.
    He wants to kill me, he told her,
        looking over his shoulder.

3 a.m. and in her nightgown, Dad asleep,
What's going on? she asked, *Who wants to kill you?*
    He looked over his shoulder.
        The devil does. Look at him, over there.

She asked, *What are you on? Who wants to kill you?*
The sky wasn't black or blue but the green of a dying night.
    The devil, look at him, over there.
        He pointed to the corner house.

The sky wasn't black or blue but the dying green of night.
Stars had closed their eyes or sheathed their knives.
    My brother pointed to the corner house.
        His lips flickered with sores.

Stars had closed their eyes or sheathed their knives.
O God, I can see the tail, he said. *O God, look.*

 Mom winced at the sores on his lips.

  It's sticking out from behind the house.

O God, see the tail, he said. *Look at the goddamned tail.*
He sat cross-legged, weeping on the front steps.

 Mom finally saw it, a hellish vision, my brother.

  O God, O God, she said.

Reverse Suicide

The guy Dad sold your car to
comes back to get his money,

leaves the car. With filthy rags
we rub it down until it doesn't shine

and wipe your blood into
the seams of the seat.

Each snowflake stirs before
lifting into the sky as I

learn you won't be dead.
The unsuffering ends

when the mess of your head
pulls together around

a bullet in your mouth.
You spit it into Dad's gun

before arriving in the driveway
while the evening brightens

and we pour bag after bag
of leaves on the lawn,

waiting for them to leap
onto the bare branches.

Charlottesville Nocturne

The late September night is a train of thought, a wound
That doesn't bleed, dead grass that's still green,
No off-shoots, no elegance,
                     the late September night,
Deprived of adjectives, abstraction's utmost and gleam.

It has been said there is an end to the giving out of names.
It has been said that everything that's written has grown hollow.
It has been said that scorpions dance where language falters and
    gives way.
It has been said that something shines out from every darkness,
                        that something shines out.

Leaning against the invisible, we bend and nod.
Evening arranges itself around the fallen leaves
Alphabetized across the backyard,
                     desolate syllables
That braille us and sign us, leaning against the invisible.

Our dreams are luminous, a cast fire upon the world.
Morning arrives and that's it.
                   Sunlight darkens the earth.

Downhearted

Six horses died in a tractor-trailer fire.
There. That's the hard part. I wanted
to tell you straight away so we could
grieve together. So many sad things,
that's just one on a long recent list
that loops and elongates in the chest,
in the diaphragm, in the alveoli. What
is it they say, *heartsick* or *downhearted*?
I picture a heart lying down on the floor
of the torso, pulling up the blankets
over its head, thinking this pain will
go on forever (even though it won't).
The heart is watching Lifetime movies
and wishing, and missing all the good
parts of her that she has forgotten.
The heart is so tired of beating
herself up, she wants to stop it still,
but also she wants the blood to return,
wants to bring in the thrill and wind of the ride,
the fast pull of life driving underneath her.
What the heart wants? The heart wants
her horses back.

becoming a horse

It was dragging my hands along its belly,
loosing the bit and wiping the spit
from its mouth made me
a snatch of grass in the thing's maw,
a fly tasting its ear. It was
touching my nose to his made me know
the clover's bloom, my wet eye to his
made me know the long field's secrets.
But it was putting my heart to the horse's that made me know
the sorrow of horses. The sorrow
of a brook creasing a field. The maggot
turning in its corpse. Made me
forsake my thumbs for the sheen of unshod hooves.
And in this way drop my torches.
And in this way drop my knives.
Feel the small song in my chest
swell and my coat glisten and twitch.
And my face grow long.
And these words cast off, at last,
for the slow honest tongue of horses.

After the Diagnosis

No remembering now
when the apple sapling was blown
almost out of the ground.
No telling how,
with all the other trees around,
it alone was struck.
It must have been luck,
he thought for years, so close
to the house it grew.
It must have been night.
Change is a thing one sleeps through
when young, and he was young.
If there was a weakness in the earth,
a give he went down on his knees
to find and feel the limits of,
there is no longer.
If there was one random blow from above
the way he's come to know
from years in this place,
the roots were stronger.
Whatever the case,
he has watched this tree survive
wind ripping at his roof for nights
on end, heats and blights
that left little else alive.
No remembering now . . .
A day's changes mean all to him

and all days come down
to one clear pane
through which he sees
among all the other trees
this leaning, clenched, unyielding one
that seems cast
in the form of a blast
that would have killed it,
as if something at the heart of things,
and with the heart of things,
had willed it.

Heart/mind

A bear batting at a beehive, how

clumsy the mind
always was with the heart. Wanting
what it wanted.

The blizzard's
accountant, how
timidly the heart approached the business
of the mind. Counting
what it counted.

Light inside a cage, the way the heart—

Bird trapped in an airport, the way the mind—

How it flashed on the floor of the phone booth, my
last dime. And

this letter
I didn't send
how surprising

to find it now.

All this love I must have felt.

III. WORDS TANGLED IN DEBRIS

Who's Who

You wake up from a nap.
Your mouth feels like a cheap acrylic sweater.
You blink online and 3-D images hopscotch around you.
A telenovela actress hides under your lampshade.
You switch to voice activation.
Good Afternoon! Sings the voice of Gregory Peck.
You look out your window, across the street.
Faded mattresses sag against a chain-link fence.
The mattress seller sits on a crate, clipping his fingernails.
You think of inviting him in.
You do a scan.
Gregory Peck booms: Dwayne Healey, 28, convicted felon of
     petty larceny.
You don't know what to do so you pet your ceramic cat.
What? You ask. What? You want to go out? Well you can't.
You hear a chime.
It is your former employer informing you that they cannot release
your husband's password due to the Privacy Policy.
It is the 98th auto reply.
You bite your hand.
You check in on your husband.
After your husband went on roam, you received one message
     from him:
I am by a pond and a coyote is eating a frog. It's amazing.
You decide to go outside.
You walk to the public park.

There is a track where people run while watching whatever
they're watching.
You sit on an oversized bench.
You think of your old town house with the oatmeal sofa
before you and husband downgraded to this neighborhood.
The sofa made you happy.
You decide you need to keep up appearances.
You need to clip your husband's nails. They are getting long.
A strangled *yip* escapes from you and a jogger stares at you.
You see a palm tree and it is carved up with little penis drawings.
You make a sound like tut-tut.
You enhance the park.
You fill in the balding grass and rub the offensive drawings
from the tree. You add coconuts.
You feel your insides are being squeezed out through a tiny hole
the size of a mosquito bite.
You hear children laughing as they rush out of a bus and it sounds
far away and watery, like how it used to in the movies, when the
    light was haloey,
and it was slow-motion, and the actor was having a terrible
    flashback.
But you are not having a flashback.
Underneath the sound of children laughing, you hear users
    chatting
over each other, which all blurs into a warring shadow of insects
and the one that sounds like a hornet is your husband,
telling you to put his stuff in storage.
Or sell it to pay off bills or
leave, why don't you goddamn leave.

You sit on the bench until the sky turns pink.
When your former employer let you go,
they said, you are now free to pursue what you want to pursue.
So here you are.

Minimum Wage

My mother and I are on the front porch lighting each other's
     cigarettes
as if we were on a ten-minute break from our jobs
at being a mother and son, just ten minutes
to steal a moment of freedom before clocking back in, before
putting the aprons back on, the paper hats,
washing our hands twice and then standing
behind the counter again,
hoping for tips, hoping the customers
will be nice, will say some kind word, the cool
front yard before us and the dogs
in the backyard shitting on everything.
We are hunched over, two extras on the set of *The Night of
     the Hunter.*
I am pulling a second cigarette out of the pack, a swimmer
rising from a pool of other swimmers. Soon we will go back
inside and sit in the yellow kitchen and drink
the rest of the coffee
and what is coming to kill us will pour milk
into mine and sugar into hers.

Proximities

A man walks into a coffee shop.
But it's not a joke.
I bought coffee there
last summer.
Small, with milk.
It's never a joke
to walk in or out of a shop
unharmed. It's easy
to forget
you aren't a person
being shot at.
I'm not.
I wasn't, though
I was there
last summer.
Not-shot-at
and I never knew it.
Did not once
think it.
Thinking it now
the moment thins,
it sheers
and I move back
to other coffee shops
where I never fell, or bled,
and then

I sit for a while
with my regular cup
and feel things collapse
or go on, I can't tell.

Story of Girls

Years ago, my brothers took turns holding down a girl in a room.
They weren't doing anything to her but they were laughing and
sometimes it's the laughing that does enough. They held the girl
   down

for an hour and she was crying, her mouth stuffed with a small
   red cloth.
Their laughing matched her crying in the same pitch. That marriage
of sound was an error and the error kept repeating itself.

There were threats of putting her in the closet or in the basement
if she didn't quiet down. One cousin told them to stop but no
   one could
hear him above the high roar. After that the boy was silent,
   looking down

at his hands, gesturing toward the locked door. The mother was
   able
to push the door in and the boys were momentarily ashamed,
   remembering
for the first time that the girl was their younger sister. The
   mother ran

to the girl fearful that something had been damaged. Nothing
   was touched.
The brothers were merely dismissed as they jostled each other
   down

the long staircase. The girl sat up to breathe a little, then a little
more.

Oftentimes it's the quiet cousin I think about.

Fourth Grade Autobiography

We live in Los Angeles, California.
We have a front yard and a backyard.
My favorite things are cartwheels, salted plums,
and playing catch with my dad. I squeeze the grass
and dirt between my fingers. Eat my tongue
white. He launches every ball into orbit.
Every ball drops like an anvil, heavy
and straight into my hands. I am afraid
of riots and falling and the dark.
The sunset of flames ringing our block,
groceries and Asian-owned storefronts. No one
to catch me. Midnight walks from his room to mine.
I believe in the devil.
I have a sister and a brother
and a strong headlock. We have a dog named
Spunky, fawn and black. We have an olive
tree. A black walnut tree. A fig tree.
We lie in the grass and wonder who writes
in the sky. I lie in the grass and imagine
my name, a cloud drifting. Saturday
dance parties. Everyone drunk on pink
panties, screw drivers, and Canadian Club.
Dominoes and spades. Al Green and Mack 10.
Sometimes Mama dances with the dog.
Sometimes my dad dances with me. I am
careful not to touch. He is careful
to smile with his whole face.

No

Yes, that was me you saw shaking with bravery, with a government-issued rifle on my back. I'm sorry I could not greet you, as you deserved, my relative.

They were not my tears. I have a reservoir inside. They will be cried by my sons, my daughters if I can't learn how to turn tears to stone.

Yes, that was me, standing in the back door of the house in the alley, with fresh corn and bread for the neighbors.

I did not foresee the flood of blood. How they would forget our friendship, would return to kill the babies and me.

Yes, that was me whirling on the dance floor. We made such a racket with all that joy. I loved the whole world in that silly music.

I did not realize the terrible dance in the staccato of bullets.

Yes. I smelled the burning grease of corpses. And like a fool I expected our words might rise up and jam the artillery in the hands of dictators.

We had to keep going. We sang our grief to clean the air of turbulent spirits.

Yes, I did see the terrible black clouds as I cooked dinner. And the messages of the dying spelled there in the ashy sunset. Every one addressed: "mother."

There was nothing about it in the news. Everything was the same. Unemployment was up. Another queen crowned with flowers. Then there were the sports scores.

Yes, the distance was great between your country and mine. Yet our children played in the path between our houses.

No. We had no quarrel with each other.

The Long Deployment

For weeks, I breathe his body in the sheet
         and pillow. I lift a blanket to my face.
There's bitter incense paired with something sweet,
         like sandalwood left sitting in the heat
or cardamom rubbed on a piece of lace.
         For weeks, I breathe his body. In the sheet
I smell anise, the musk that we secrete
         with longing, leather and moss. I find a trace
of bitter incense paired with something sweet.
         Am I imagining the wet scent of peat
and cedar, oud, impossible to erase?
         For weeks, I breathe his body in the sheet—
crushed pepper—although perhaps discreet,
         difficult for someone else to place.
There's bitter incense paired with something sweet.
         With each deployment I become an aesthete
of smoke and oak. Patchouli fills the space
         for weeks. I breathe his body in the sheet
until he starts to fade, made incomplete,
         a bottle almost empty in its case.
There's bitter incense paired with something sweet.
         And then he's gone. Not even the conceit
of him remains, not the resinous base.
         For weeks, I breathed his body in the sheet.
He was bitter incense paired with something sweet.

FROM *Personal Effects*

Daily I sit
with the language
they've made

of our language

to NEUTRALIZE
the CAPABILITY of LOW DOLLAR VALUE ITEMS
like you.

You are what is referred to as
a "CASUALTY." Unclear whether
from a CATALYTIC or FRONTAL ATTACK, unclear

the final time you were addressed

thou, beloved. It was for us a
CATASTROPHIC EVENT.

Just, DESTROYED.

DIED OF WOUND RECEIVED IN ACTION.

Yes, there was
EARLY WARNING.
You said you were especially scared
of mortar rounds.

In EXECUTION PLANNING, they weighed
the losses, the SUSTAINABILITY
and budgeted

for X number,
they budgeted for the phone call
to your mother and weighed that

against the amount saved in rations
and your taste for cigarettes

and the tea you poured your boys
and the tea you would've poured me
approaching *Hello*.

The change you collected in jars
jumping a bit
as the family learns to slam
the home's various doors.

We Lived Happily during the War

And when they bombed other people's houses, we

protested
but not enough, we opposed them but not

enough. I was
in my bed, around my bed America

was falling: invisible house by invisible house by invisible house—

I took a chair outside and watched the sun.

In the sixth month
of a disastrous reign in the house of money

in the street of money in the city of money in the country of money,
our great country of money, we (forgive us)

lived happily during the war.

Phantom Noise

There is this ringing hum   this
bullet-borne language   ringing
shell-fall and static this   late-night
ringing of threadwork and carpet   ringing
hiss and steam   this wing-beat
of rotors and tanks   broken
bodies ringing in steel   humming these
voices of dust   these years ringing
rifles in Babylon   rifles in Sumer
ringing these children their gravestones
and candy   their limbs gone missing   their
static-borne television   their ringing
this eardrum   this rifled symphonic   this
ringing of midnight in gunpowder and oil   this
brake pad gone useless   this muzzle-flash singing   this
threading of bullets in muscle and bone   this ringing
hum   this ringing hum   this
ringing

Ten Drumbeats to God

I confess to stealing the tomb to bury my mother. I admit to emptying the gas tank my neighbor kept for *blakawout*. I took the rope and the cakes of an old lady because she had more and I needed some. I stole a radio to eat. Stole medicine to sleep. I tried to forget I lay beside dead bodies but my eyes couldn't shut. Tried to refill my heart but it stayed shut. I wished and wish some more to be dead and not an idea, a solitude, a shame. I summoned words tangled in debris, measured the distance of fire a mile into my voice. I took everything and a little more. Then I heard the drumbeats and remembered—like rain like song like light lit by old questions—there is no reason, there is god, drum, beat. there is what lingers and there is what comes later.

IV. HERE,
THE SENTENCE WILL BE RESPECTED

38

Here, the sentence will be respected.

I will compose each sentence with care, by minding what the rules of writing dictate.

For example, all sentences will begin with capital letters.

Likewise, the history of the sentence will be honored by ending each one with appropriate punctuation such as a period or question mark, thus bringing the idea to (momentary) completion.

You may like to know, I do not consider this a "creative piece."

I do not regard this as a poem of great imagination or a work of fiction.

Also, historical events will not be dramatized for an "interesting" read.

Therefore, I feel most responsible to the orderly sentence; conveyor of thought.

That said, I will begin.

You may or may not have heard about the Dakota 38.

If this is the first time you've heard of it, you might wonder, "What is the Dakota 38?"

The Dakota 38 refers to thirty-eight Dakota men who were executed by hanging, under orders from President Abraham Lincoln.

To date, this is the largest "legal" mass execution in US history.

The hanging took place on December 26, 1862—the day after Christmas.

This was the *same week* that President Lincoln signed the Emancipation Proclamation.

In the preceding sentence, I italicize "same week" for emphasis.

There was a movie titled *Lincoln* about the presidency of Abraham Lincoln.

The signing of the Emancipation Proclamation was included in the film *Lincoln*; the hanging of the Dakota 38 was not.

In any case, you might be asking, "Why were thirty-eight Dakota men hung?"

As a side note, the past tense of hang is *hung*, but when referring to the capital punishment of hanging, the correct past tense is *hanged*.

So it's possible that you're asking, "Why were thirty-eight Dakota men hanged?"

They were hanged for the Sioux Uprising.

I want to tell you about the Sioux Uprising, but I don't know where to begin.

I may jump around and details will not unfold in chronological order.

Keep in mind, I am not a historian.

So I will recount facts as best as I can, given limited resources and understanding.

Before Minnesota was a state, the Minnesota region, generally speaking, was the traditional homeland for Dakota, Anishinaabeg, and Ho-Chunk people.

During the 1800s, when the US expanded territory, they "purchased" land from the Dakota people as well as the other tribes.

But another way to understand that sort of "purchase" is: Dakota leaders ceded land to the US government in exchange for money or goods, but most importantly, the safety of their people.

Some say that Dakota leaders did not understand the terms they were entering, or they never would have agreed.

Even others call the entire negotiation "trickery."

But to make whatever-it-was official and binding, the US government drew up an initial treaty.

This treaty was later replaced by another (more convenient) treaty, and then another.

I've had difficulty unraveling the terms of these treaties, given the legal speak and congressional language.

As treaties were abrogated (broken) and new treaties were drafted, one after another, the new treaties often referenced old defunct treaties, and it is a muddy, switchback trail to follow.

Although I often feel lost on this trail, I know I am not alone.

However, as best as I can put the facts together, in 1851, Dakota territory was contained to a twelve-mile by one-hundred-fifty-mile-long strip along the Minnesota River.

But just seven years later, in 1858, the northern portion was ceded (taken) and the southern portion was (conveniently) allotted, which reduced Dakota land to a stark ten-mile tract.

These amended and broken treaties are often referred to as the Minnesota Treaties.

The word *Minnesota* comes from *mni*, which means water; and *sota*, which means turbid.

Synonyms for turbid include muddy, unclear, cloudy, confused, and smoky.

Everything is in the language we use.

For example, a treaty is, essentially, a contract between two sovereign nations.

The US treaties with the Dakota Nation were legal contracts that promised money.

It could be said, this money was payment for the land the Dakota ceded; for living within assigned boundaries (a reservation); and for relinquishing rights to their vast hunting territory which, in turn, made Dakota people dependent on other means to survive: money.

The previous sentence is circular, akin to so many aspects of history.

As you may have guessed by now, the money promised in the turbid treaties did not make it into the hands of Dakota people.

In addition, local government traders would not offer credit to "Indians" to purchase food or goods.

Without money, store credit, or rights to hunt beyond their ten-mile tract of land, Dakota people began to starve.

The Dakota people were starving.

The Dakota people starved.

In the preceding sentence, the word "starved" does not need italics for emphasis.

One should read "The Dakota people starved" as a straightforward and plainly stated fact.

As a result—and without other options but to continue to starve—Dakota people retaliated.

Dakota warriors organized, struck out, and killed settlers and traders.

This revolt is called the Sioux Uprising.

Eventually, the US Cavalry came to Mnisota to confront the Uprising.

More than one thousand Dakota people were sent to prison.

As already mentioned, thirty-eight Dakota men were subsequently hanged.

After the hanging, those one thousand Dakota prisoners were released.

However, as further consequence, what remained of Dakota territory in Mnisota was dissolved (stolen).

The Dakota people had no land to return to.

This means they were exiled.

Homeless, the Dakota people of Mnisota were relocated (forced) onto reservations in South Dakota and Nebraska.

Now, every year, a group called the Dakota 38 + 2 Riders conduct a memorial horse ride from Lower Brule, South Dakota, to Mankato, Mnisota.

The Memorial Riders travel 325 miles on horseback for eighteen days, sometimes through sub-zero blizzards.

They conclude their journey on December 26, the day of the hanging.

Memorials help focus our memory on particular people or events.

Often, memorials come in the forms of plaques, statues, or gravestones.

The memorial for the Dakota 38 is not an object inscribed with words, but an *act*.

Yet, I started this piece because I was interested in writing about grasses.

So, there is one other event to include, although it's not in chronological order and we must backtrack a little.

When the Dakota people were starving, as you may remember, government traders would not extend store credit to "Indians."

One trader named Andrew Myrick is famous for his refusal to provide credit to Dakota people by saying, "If they are hungry, let them eat grass."

There are variations of Myrick's words, but they are all something to that effect.

When settlers and traders were killed during the Sioux Uprising, one of the first to be executed by the Dakota was Andrew Myrick.

When Myrick's body was found,

                              his mouth was stuffed with grass.

I am inclined to call this act by the Dakota warriors a poem.

There's irony in their poem.

There was no text.

"Real" poems do not "really" require words.

I have italicized the previous sentence to indicate inner dialogue, a revealing moment.

But, on second thought, the words "Let them eat grass" click the gears of the poem into place.

So, we could also say, language and word choice are crucial to the poem's work.

Things are circling back again.

Sometimes, when in a circle, if I wish to exit, I must leap.

And let the body   swing.

From the platform.

                         Out

                                        to the grasses.

V. ONE SINGING THING

Elegy

> For my father

I think by now the river must be thick
> with salmon. Late August, I imagine it

as it was that morning: drizzle needling
> the surface, mist at the banks like a net

settling around us—everything damp
> and shining. That morning, awkward

and heavy in our hip waders, we stalked
> into the current and found our places—

you upstream a few yards and out
> far deeper. You must remember how

the river seeped in over your boots
> and you grew heavier with that defeat.

All day I kept turning to watch you, how
> first you mimed our guide's casting

then cast your invisible line, slicing the sky
> between us; and later, rod in hand, how

you tried—again and again—to find
> that perfect arc, flight of an insect

skimming the river's surface. Perhaps
    you recall I cast my line and reeled in

two small trout we could not keep.
    Because I had to release them, I confess,

I thought about the past—working
    the hooks loose, the fish writhing

in my hands, each one slipping away
    before I could let go. I can tell you now

that I tried to take it all in, record it
    for an elegy I'd write—one day—

when the time came. Your daughter,
    I was that ruthless. What does it matter

if I tell you I *learned* to be? You kept casting
    your line, and when it did not come back

empty, it was tangled with mine. Some nights,
    dreaming, I step again into the small boat

that carried us out and watch the bank receding—
    my back to where I know we are headed.

Object Permanence
[For John]

We wake as if surprised the other is still there,
each petting the sheet to be sure.

How we have managed our way
to this bed—beholden to heat like dawn

indebted to light. Though we're not so self-
important as to think everything

has led to this, everything has led to this.
There's a name for the animal

love makes of us—named, I think,
like rain, for the sound it makes.

You are the animal after whom other animals
are named. Until there's none left to laugh,

days will start with the same startle
and end with caterpillars gorged on milkweed.

O, how we entertain the angels
with our brief animation. O,

how I'll miss you when we're dead.

Crowning

Now that knowing means nothing,
now that you are more born
than being, more awake
than awaited, since I've seen
your hair deep inside mother,
a glimpse, grass in late
winter, early spring, watching
your mother's pursed, throbbing,
purpled power, her pushing
you for one whole hour, two,
almost three, almost out,
maybe never, animal smell
and peat, breath and sweat
and mulch-matter, and at once
you descend, or drive, are driven
by mother's body, by her will
and brilliance, by bowel,
by wanting and your hair
peering as if it could see, and I saw
you storming forth,
taproot, your cap of hair half
in, half out, and *wait, hold
it there*, the doctors say, and
she squeezing my hand, her face
full of fire, then groaning your face
out like a flower, blood-bloom,
crocused into air, shoulders

and the long cord still rooting
you to each other, to the other
world, into this afterlife
among us living, the cord
I cut like an iris, pulsing,
then you wet against mother's chest
still purple, not blue, not yet
red, no cry,
warming now, now opening
your eyes midnight
blue in the blue black dawn.

Hurricane

Four tickets left, I let her go—
Firstborn into a hurricane.

I thought she escaped
The floodwaters. No—but her

Head is empty of the drowned
For now—though she took

Her first breath below sea level.
Ahhh   awe   &   aw
Mama, let me go—she speaks

What every smart child knows—
To get grown you unlatch

Your hands from the grown
& up & up & up & up
She turns—latched in the seat

Of a hurricane. (You let
Your girl what? You let

Your girl what?)
I did so she do I did
So she do so—

Girl, you can ride
A hurricane & she do
& she do & she do & she do

She do make my river
An ocean. Memorial.
Baptist. Protestant. Birth—my girl

Walked away from a hurricane.
& she do & she do & she do & she do
She do take my hand a while longer.

The haunts in my pocket
I'll keep to a hum: *Katrina was*
A woman I knew. When you were

An infant she rained on you & she

do & she do & she do & she do

*Requiem for Fifth Period
   and the Things That Went On Then*

Sing, muse, of the science teacher
looking wearily at the stack of ungraded projects
leaning against the back wall, beneath a board on which
she has hastily drawn a pinnate leaf and a palmate leaf
with a violet dry erase marker.
She moves from her desk to the window to watch the flag
   football game
and the man in the electric wheelchair leaving the senior housing
   complex
and an old Lincoln Town Car parked near the tremendous
   pothole that damaged her axle that morning
and the White Castle bag moving in a sudden gust across the
   basketball court, as if possessed
and Mr. Harris, blowing his whistle.

Tell us of Javonte Stevens, who is in the fourth grade
and who is now tapping Mr. Harris on the shoulder to say
that Miss Kaizer will be sending over three kids
who did not bring in their field trip money
and cannot go to the aquarium
and is that okay.
Sing of Javonte's new glasses,
their black frames and golden hinges that glint in the sun,
and his new haircut, with two notched arrows shorn above his
   temples

and his new socks which are hidden but which feel best of all
and which were the last of the new things he received from his
    auntie this weekend
when she visited from Detroit and slept on the couch and
    declared that
Javonte's improved grades meant that he should have many new
    things.
Sing of the rough-hewn piece of wood Javonte used
to keep the heavy door ajar while he was outside.
Call out
the noise it made against the painted cement when he kicked it
    back in.
Sing the song Javonte hummed as he carried his message
back up the stairs, stepping in tune, nodding in tune
to Bo as she called after him,
warning him not to slip on the newly mopped floor.

Sing, muse, of Bo, moving the mop
from the top of the ramp to the bottom,
stepping gingerly past the place where the carpet's unruly corner
    bends upward,
guiding the wheels of the bucket to stay unwillingly upright
despite the heavy dent in the one.
Speak of the pungent, alkaline smell of the water
and the slap when the fibers hit the floor
and the squeal of the bathroom door
and the shuddering sob,
audible in the moment that disc two of *The Broker* by John Grisham

skips in Bo's CD player,
and her pause in the threshold
and her retreat to the boys' room, which can be cleaned first.

Tell of Nakyla Smith, breathing in sharply when the bathroom
     door closes,
pushing the stall open gently, silently moving to the sink,
splashing water on her face and wiping her eyes
with the sleeve of her blue oxford.
Sing of her heavy ascent to the counselor's office,
for today is the day
she will unbutton her collar, and the button below, and the
     button below,
and tug aside the bleached white tank top
to show the small, round burns that pepper her breast.
Praise Ms. Hightower, who does not gasp or cry out at the
     moment of revelation,
only holds one brown hand in her own
and with her left, lifts the phone and dials Mrs. Marshall,
though she is only just across the hall.

Sing, muse, of Mrs. Marshall, who cannot answer now.
The desk is unattended and she leans
against the other side of the oaken door,
the principal's side, where a sign reads "Children Are My Business"
and a doll-like painted woman smiles broadly, surrounded by the
     faces of earnest pupils.
She is resting against the wood as her forearms strain
with the weight of all the papers,

colored like oatmeal or dust, each with a label at the top.
The first says STEVENS, JAVONTE, and below that, KAIZER,
and below that, eight numbers.
Tell of how she collates them by classroom, then alphabetically,
though each letter is the same, though each bears the same news.

Tell, muse, of the siren that called their joy sparse and their love
    vacant.
Tell of the wind that scattered them.

Dear P.

Someone will   love you   many will   love

you   many will brother you   some of these

loves will   bother you   some   will   leave you

one might   haunt   you   hunt you in your

sleep   make you   weep the tearless kind of

weep the   kind of weep   that drowns your

organs   slowly   there are little oars   in your body

little boats   grab onto them and row and   row

someone will tell you   *no*   but you won't   know

he is   right until you have   already   wrung your

own heart dry   your hands dripping knives   until

you have   already   reached your hands into   his

body and put them through his   heart   love is

the only thing that   is not   an   argument

Lines for Little Mila

Here, in a cloud of rising flour
she dabs at her chin—   aging
leaves a blemish just like this . . .
the egg behind the cloud
of flour now falling
to a black mica counter.

Grandmother with a coffee tin
full of raw milk. The sun
gone beyond the mountains
long before it's gone from us.

Men cleaning fish, husking
corn on the porch.

I told a friend's little girl
about some of this,
and she immediately
slumbered, putting
a blue ghost inside my chest.

I said to her—
so you still remember things from the other side?
Then quickly I added—

of that river?

Mercy

Like two wrestlers etched
around some ancient urn

we'd lace our hands,
then wrench

each other's wrists back
until the muscles ached

and the tendons burned,
and one brother

or the other grunted *Mercy*—
a game we played

so many times
I finally taught my sons,

not knowing what it was,
until too late, I'd done:

when the oldest rose
like my brother's ghost,

grappling the little
ghost I was at ten—

who cried out *Mercy!*
in my own voice *Mercy!*

as I watched from deep
inside my father's skin.

Apparition

I'm carrying an orange plastic basket of compost
down from the top of the garden—sweet dark,

fibrous rot, promising—when the light changes
as if someone's flipped a switch that does

what? Reverses the day. Leaves chorusing,
dizzy. And then my mother says

—she's been gone more than thirty years,
not her voice, the voice of her in me—

You've got to forgive me. I'm choke and sputter
in the wild daylight, speechless to that:

maybe I'm really crazy now, but I believe
in the backwards morning I am my mother's son,

we are at last equally in love
with intoxication, I am unregenerate,

the trees are on fire, fifty-eight years of lost bells.
I drop my basket and stand struck

in the iron-mouth afternoon. She says
I never meant to harm you. Then

the young dog barks, down by the front gate,
he's probably gotten out, and she says,

calmly, clearly, *Go take care of your baby.*

At Pegasus

They are like those crazy women
    who tore Orpheus
        when he refused to sing,

these men grinding
    in the strobe & black lights
        of Pegasus. All shadow & sound.

"I'm just here for the music,"
    I tell the man who asks me
        to the floor. But I have held

a boy on my back before.
    Curtis & I used to leap
        barefoot into the creek; dance

among maggots & piss,
    beer bottles & tadpoles
        slippery as sperm;

we used to pull off our shirts,
    & slap music into our skin.
        He wouldn't know me now

at the edge of these lovers' gyre,
    glitter & steam, fire,
        bodies blurred sexless

by the music's spinning light.
    A young man slips his thumb
        into the mouth of an old one,

& I am not that far away.
    The whole scene raw & delicate
        as Curtis's foot gashed

on a sunken bottle shard.
    They press hip to hip,
        each breathless as a boy

carrying a friend on his back.
    The foot swelling green
        as the sewage in that creek.

We never went back.
    But I remember his weight
        better than I remember

my first kiss.
    These men know something
        I used to know.

How could I not find them
    beautiful, the way they dive & spill
        into each other,

the way the dance floor
    takes them,
        wet & holy in its mouth.

Scorch Marks

Whenever we find wide black swaths burned across our paths
We think of you. Our friend the black swan turns to look
At us frequently when we pass by its pond. We see your back
Far away deep inside the pupils of those we love. We stare
And we stare where we are. That is what we do. It makes us
Look as if we've misplaced our minds or perhaps replaced
Ideas of mind with some new stronger fog. I feel you
Fading and find you falling for that feeling, you staring farther
Into one of the farthest vanishing points in the universe.
We find this alarming. We are losing track of something.
Our friend the black dog watches us carefully as we walk by
The door she guards. The crows look at us in their crooked
Ways. They converse and inverse and walk like the mechanics
Of mystery they are. Who are we to believe what we say?

Dog Talk

We-be   bo-broke   e-bev-ry-by
sy-byl-la-ba-ble-ble

O-bour   mo-bouths   bo-broke   the-bem
an-band   o-bo-pe-bened   the-bem
fo-bor   ai-bair   o-bor   wa-ba-ter-ber
o-bor   see-beed   o-bor   foo-bood.

A-banse-se-bers,   que-bues-tio-bens,
na-bames,   se-be-cre-bets.   We-be
be-bent   E-ben-gli-bish,
em-bem-bra-braced   i-bit
the-ben   e-be-ra-based   i-bit
a-bat   the-be   sa-bame   ti-bime.

Romanticism 101

Then I realized I hadn't secured the boat.
Then I realized my friend had lied to me.
Then I realized my dog was gone
no matter how much I called in the rain.
All was change.
Then I realized I was surrounded by aliens
disguised as orthodontists having a convention
at the hotel breakfast bar.
Then I could see into the life of things,
that systems seek only to reproduce
the conditions of their own reproduction.
If I had to pick between shadows
and essences, I'd pick shadows.
They're better dancers.
They always sing their telegrams.
Their old gods do not die.
Then I realized the very futility was salvation
in this greeny entanglement of breaths.
Yeah, as if.
Then I realized even when you catch the mechanism,
the trick still convinces.
Then I came to in Texas
and realized rockabilly would never go away.
Then I realized I'd been drugged.
We were all chasing nothing
which left no choice but to intensify the chase.
I came to handcuffed and gagged.

I came to intubated and packed in some kind of foam.
This too is how ash moves through water.
And all this time the side door unlocked.
Then I realized repetition could be an ending.
Then I realized repetition could be an ending.

For the Last American Buffalo

After a photograph by Richard Sherman

Because words dazzle in the dizzy light of things
and the soul is like an animal—hunted and slow—
this buffalo walks through me every night as if I was
some kind of prairie and hunkers against the cold dark,
snorting under the stars while the fog of its breathing
rises in the air, and it is the loneliest feeling I know
to approach it slowly with my hand outstretched
to tenderly touch the heavy skull furred and rough
and stroke that place huge between its ears where
what I think and what it thinks are one singing thing
so quiet that, when I wake, I seldom remember
walking beside it and whispering in its ear quietly
passing the miles, the two of us, as if Cheyenne or
the lights of San Francisco were our unlikely destination
and sometimes trains pass us and no one leans out hard
in the dark aiming to end us and so we continue on
somehow and today while the seismic quietness of
the earth spun beneath my feet and while the world
I guess carried on, that lumbering thing moved heavy
thick and dark through the dreams I believe we keep
having whether we sleep or not and when you see it
again say *I'm sorry* for things you didn't do and
then offer it some sweet-grass and tell it stories
you remember from the star-chamber of the womb
or at least the latest joke, something good to keep it
company as otherwise it doesn't know you are here
for love, and like the world tonight, doesn't really
care whether we live or die. Tell it you do and why.

JAN BEATTY is the author of *Jackknife: New and Selected Poems*, and was named by the *Huffington Post* as one of ten women writers for "required reading." She lives in Pittsburgh, Pennsylvania.

JERICHO BROWN is the author of *The New Testament* and *Please*. He teaches in the creative writing program at Emory University and lives in Atlanta, Georgia.

TINA CHANG is the author of *Half-Lit Houses* and *Of Gods & Strangers*, and is coeditor of *Language for a New Century: Contemporary Poetry from the Middle East, Asia, and Beyond*. She lives in Brooklyn, New York.

VICTORIA CHANG's poetry collections include *Circle*, *Salvinia Molesta*, *The Boss*, and *Barbie Chang*. She lives in Southern California.

OLIVER DE LA PAZ is the author of four poetry collections, *Names above Houses*, *Furious Lullaby*, *Requiem for the Orchard*, and *Post Subject: A Fable*. He teaches at the College of the Holy Cross and in the low-residency MFA program at Pacific Lutheran University. He lives in Massachusetts.

NATALIE DIAZ was born and raised in the Fort Mojave Indian Village in Needles, California. She is Mojave and an enrolled member of the Gila River Indian Tribe. Diaz teaches at Arizona State University, and her first poetry collection is *When My Brother Was an Aztec*.

MATTHEW DICKMAN is the author of *All-American Poem*, *Mayakovsky's Revolver*, and *Wonderland*. He lives in Portland, Oregon.

MARK DOTY is a poet, essayist, and memoirist. He is the author of ten books of poetry, including *Deep Lane* and *Fire to Fire: New and Selected Poems*, which won the National Book Award. He lives in New York, New York.

NORMAN DUBIE is the author of twenty-eight collections of poetry, most recently *The Quotations of Bone*, which won the Griffin Poetry Prize. He lives and teaches in Tempe, Arizona.

JEHANNE DUBROW is the author of six books of poetry, including *Dots & Dashes*, *Red Army Red*, and *Stateside*. She is an associate professor of creative writing at the University of North Texas.

EVE L. EWING is a poet, essayist, sociologist, and educator. *Electric Arches* is her first book of poetry. She lives in Chicago, Illinois.

VIEVEE FRANCIS is the author of *Blue-Tail Fly*, *Horse in the Dark*, and *Forest Primeval*, which won the Kingsley Tufts Poetry Award and the Hurston/Wright Legacy Award in Poetry. She teaches at Dartmouth College.

ROSS GAY is the author of *Catalog of Unabashed Gratitude*, winner of the National Book Critics Circle Award and the Kingsley Tufts Poetry Award. He teaches at Indiana University.

ARACELIS GIRMAY is the author of three collections of poetry, including *Teeth*, *Kingdom Animalia*, and *The Black Maria*. Originally from California, she lives with her family in New York, New York.

NATHALIE HANDAL is the author of five books of poetry, including *The Republics* and *Poet in Andalucía*. She is a professor at Columbia University and lives in New York, New York.

JOY HARJO is the author of eight books of poetry, most recently *Conflict Resolution for Holy Beings*. She was recently awarded the Ruth Lilly Prize for lifetime achievement in poetry from the Poetry Foundation. She is a member of the Muscogee Nation and teaches at the University of Tennessee.

YONA HARVEY is the author of *Hemming the Water*, which won the Kate Tufts Discovery Award. She teaches at the University of Pittsburgh.

TERRANCE HAYES is the author of six poetry collections, including *American Sonnets for My Past and Future Assassin*, *How to Be Drawn*, and *Lighthead*, which won the National Book Award. He is a MacArthur Fellow and teaches at the University of Pittsburgh.

CATHY PARK HONG is a poet and critic whose books include *Translating Mo'um*, *Dance Dance Revolution*, and *Engine Empire*. She is a professor at Rutgers–Newark University.

MARIE HOWE is the author of four books of poetry, including *Magdalene* and *What the Living Do*. She lives in New York, New York.

MAJOR JACKSON is the author of four collections of poetry, *Roll Deep*, *Holding Company*, *Hoops*, and *Leaving Saturn*. He teaches at the University of Vermont.

ILYA KAMINSKY was born in the former Soviet Union and is now an American citizen. He is the author of two poetry books, *Deaf Republic* and *Dancing in Odessa*, and editor of *The Ecco Anthology of International Poetry*. He received a Whiting Writers' Award. He teaches at San Diego State University.

LAURA KASISCHKE teaches in the MFA program at the University of Michigan. She is the author of many books of poetry, including *Where Now: New and Selected Poems* and *Space, in Chains*, which won the National Book Critics Circle Award in Poetry. She lives in Ann Arbor, Michigan.

DONIKA KELLY's first poetry collection is *Bestiary*, winner of the Cave Canem Poetry Prize and the Kate Tufts Discovery Award. She lives in Brooklyn, New York.

ROBIN COSTE LEWIS's first book of poems, *Voyage of the Sable Venus*, won the National Book Award in Poetry. She lives and teaches in Los Angeles, California.

ADA LIMÓN is the author of five books of poetry, including *The Carrying* and *Bright Dead Things*, which was a finalist for the National Book Award. She lives in Lexington, Kentucky, and Sonoma, California.

PATRICIA LOCKWOOD is the author of two books of poetry, *Motherland Fatherland Homelandsexuals* and *Balloon Pop Outlaw Black*, and a memoir, *Priestdaddy*. She lives in Savannah, Georgia.

LAYLI LONG SOLDIER is the author of *WHEREAS*, which won the National Book Critics Circle Award and the PEN/Jean Stein Award and was a finalist for the National Book Award. She is a citizen of the Oglala Lakota Nation and lives in Santa Fe, New Mexico.

PATRICK PHILLIPS is the author of *Chattahoochee*, *Boy*, and *Elegy for a Broken Machine*, which was a finalist for the National Book Award. He lives in Brooklyn, New York.

LIA PURPURA's latest poetry collection is *It Shouldn't Have Been Beautiful*. The recipient of a Guggenheim fellowship and a finalist for the National Book Critics Circle Award, she teaches at the University of Maryland and lives in Baltimore, Maryland.

MELISSA RANGE is the author of *Horse and Rider* and *Scriptorium*. Originally from East Tennessee, she now lives in Wisconsin and teaches at Lawrence University.

MATT RASMUSSEN is the author of *Black Aperture*, winner of the Walt Whitman Award of the Academy of American Poets and a finalist for the National Book Award. He lives in Robbinsdale, Minnesota.

ERIKA L. SÁNCHEZ is the author of a poetry collection, *Lessons on Expulsion*, and a novel for young readers, *I Am Not Your Perfect Mexican Daughter*, which was a finalist for the National Book Award. She lives in Chicago, Illinois.

STEVE SCAFIDI is the author of four poetry collections, including *Sparks from a Nine-Pound Hammer* and *To the Bramble and the Briar*. He lives in Summit Point, West Virginia.

NICOLE SEALEY is the author of *Ordinary Beast* and *The Animal After Whom Other Animals Are Named*. She is the executive director of Cave Canem and lives in Brooklyn, New York.

CHARIF SHANAHAN's first poetry collection is *Into Each Room We Enter without Knowing*. He is a Stegner Fellow at Stanford University and lives in the Bay Area of California.

SOLMAZ SHARIF is the author of a poetry collection, *Look*, a finalist for the National Book Award. She is currently a lecturer at Stanford University and lives in the Bay Area of California.

DANEZ SMITH is the author of two books of poetry, *[insert] boy* and *Don't Call Us Dead*, a finalist for the National Book Award. They live in Minneapolis, Minnesota.

SUSAN STEWART is the author of six books of criticism and six collections of poetry, including *Cinder: New and Selected Poems* and *Columbarium*, which won the National Book Critics Circle Award. She teaches at Princeton University and lives in New Jersey and in Philadelphia, Pennsylvania.

MARY SZYBIST is the author of two poetry collections, *Granted* and *Incarnadine*, which won the National Book Award. She teaches at Lewis & Clark College and lives in Portland, Oregon.

NATASHA TRETHEWEY is the author of four collections of poetry, including *Thrall* and *Native Guard*, which won the Pulitzer Prize. She served as the nineteenth Poet Laureate of the United States from 2012 to 2014. She is Board of Trustees Professor at Northwestern University and lives in Evanston, Illinois.

BRIAN TURNER is a veteran of the United States Army and the author of the poetry collections *Phantom Noise* and *Here, Bullet*, as well as the memoir *My Life as a Foreign Country*. He lives in Orlando, Florida.

ELLEN BRYANT VOIGT is the author of eight collections of poetry, including *Headwaters* and *Messenger: New and Selected Poems*, which was a finalist for the National Book Award and the Pulitzer Prize. She is a MacArthur Fellow and lives in Cabot, Vermont.

SUSAN WHEELER is the author of six collections of poetry, including *Assorted Poems* and *Meme*, which was a finalist for the National Book Award. She teaches in the Creative Writing Program at Princeton University.

DARA WIER is the author of fifteen collections of poetry, including *You Good Thing* and *Selected Poems*. She is the director of the MFA Program at the University of Massachusetts, Amherst.

CHRISTIAN WIMAN is a poet, translator, and essayist. His books of poetry include *Every Riven Thing* and *Once in the West*, which was a finalist for the National Book Critics Circle Award. He teaches at Yale University and lives in New Haven, Connecticut.

CHARLES WRIGHT was named Poet Laureate of the United States in 2014. He is the author of numerous collections of poetry, including *Bye-and-Bye: Selected Late Poems*. He taught at the University of Virginia.

JOHN YAU has published more than fifty books of poetry, fiction, and art criticism, including *A Thing Among Things: The Art of Jasper Johns* and *Bijoux in the Dark*. He teaches at the Mason Gross School of the Arts (Rutgers University), and lives in New York, New York.

DEAN YOUNG is the author of many collections of poetry, including *Shock by Shock*, *Bender: New and Selected Poems*, and *Elegy on a Toy Piano*, a finalist for the Pulitzer Prize. He teaches at the University of Texas, Austin.

KEVIN YOUNG is director of The New York Public Library's Schomburg Center for Research in Black Culture and poetry editor of the *New Yorker*. He is the author of thirteen books of poetry and prose, including *Brown*, *Blue Laws: Selected & Uncollected Poems 1995–2015*, *Bunk*, a finalist for the National Book Critics Circle Award in criticism, and *Jelly Roll*, a finalist for the National Book Award in poetry.

ABOUT TRACY K. SMITH

From 2017 to 2019, Tracy K. Smith served as the 22nd Poet Laureate of the United States. She is the author of four collections of poetry, including *Wade in the Water* and *Life on Mars*, winner of the Pulitzer Prize. She is also the author of a memoir, *Ordinary Light*, which was a finalist for the National Book Award. She teaches at Princeton University and lives in New Jersey.

The text of *American Journal* is set in Adobe Caslon Pro.
Book design by Rachel Holscher. Composition by Bookmobile
Design & Digital Publisher Services, Minneapolis, Minnesota.
Manufactured by Versa Press on acid-free, 30 percent
postconsumer wastepaper.

SCHOLASTIC'S A+ GUIDE TO GOOD WRITING

DIANE TEITEL RUBINS

SCHOLASTIC INC.
New York Toronto London Auckland Sydney

Over a million junior high and high school students have used Scholastic's A+ Guides to raise their grades, do better in every subject, and *enjoy* school more. Now you can, too!

SCHOLASTIC'S A+
GUIDE TO GOOD GRADES

SCHOLASTIC'S A+
GUIDE TO GOOD WRITING

SCHOLASTIC'S A+
GUIDE TO TAKING TESTS

SCHOLASTIC'S A+
GUIDE TO GRAMMAR

SCHOLASTIC'S A+
GUIDE TO RESEARCH AND TERM PAPERS

SCHOLASTIC'S A+
GUIDE TO BOOK REPORTS

ISBN 0-590-43735-6

12 11 10 9 8 7 6 5 4 3   1 2 3/9

Printed in the U.S.A.   0

For Marc

CONTENTS

Chapter 1

GET READY, GET SET, GET YOURSELF GOING

So you have to write a composition. How do you get an idea? How do you put words down on paper? How do you make it readable? And . . . how in the world do you get an A+? With keen observation, careful planning, awareness of structure and style, plus real time and effort, it *can* be done. But if you're in the middle of a creative energy crisis of your own, read on. Good news, in the form of this book, has arrived to help.

10 TIPS TO TROUBLE-FREE WRITING

1. Think positively. The first thing you should do when approaching any school as-

1

signment is to take a deep breath and say, "I *can* do it!" Nothing, but nothing, is ever gained by screaming, crying, or tearing your hair out (except maybe a sore throat, swollen eyes, and a bald head). *Positive thinking* is a powerful psychological theory that works — not an old wives' tale or some voodoo superstition. If you feel confident that you can do something, more often than not you will. Just keep in mind that old saying, "Where there's a will, there's a way." Well, if you start by developing the will from within, you can use this book to help you to perfect the way.

2. Find a quiet place to work. Find a quiet corner in which to do your writing. If you're the kind of person who can think clearly with the stereo playing, the TV droning, and the dog barking, then congratulations, because you are in the minority. But, if you're like the majority of people who need an atmosphere that is relatively free from distractions, then it is up to you to find or make one.

If you can't resist glancing at the television set, then don't work in a room where TV is the main attraction. The same goes for a radio, stereo, or even in some cases, the refrigerator. Know what your weaknesses are and *stay away from them*!

If you share a room with a brother or sister, see if you can arrange a specific study time for the two of you. Try to agree upon a time to be used strictly for schoolwork when you both promise to be as quiet as possible, giving one another the opportunity to work undisturbed. If a time cannot be mutually agreed upon, perhaps you can go to bed half an hour later, or get up half an hour earlier in order to work.

3. Acquire self-discipline. Don't just sit back and talk about doing something — do it! No one can expect a good grade on anything that she or he threw together in minutes. Sure, there are some cases of kids who dash things off the night before and get A's, but be assured that these instances are rare. Much more common is the "night-before-it's-due-paper" that just skims by with a decent grade.

If you have a paper to write, don't squeeze it into your schedule between cheerleading practice and the Saturday night movies — *make a specific time for it.* If you must, make a list of priorities to help you organize your time better. Many of the C papers of this world would have been A's if only their creators had taken the time to revise and rewrite and think about them a little bit more. If you hurry to do something, be aware that you are cheating yourself out of doing the best possible job.

4. Stock up on supplies. Invest some of your money in a good supply of paper, pens, and pencils to keep at home. One of the absolute worst excuses to give any teacher (right behind "My dog chewed it up!") is that you ran out of paper, or couldn't find a sharp pencil or a pen that worked. Save yourself the embarrassment of having to use such a poor excuse and buy enough supplies to last at least one semester. School supplies don't spoil with time and they never go out of style.

5. Learn to type. Most teachers have not taken

a course in handwriting analysis, nor should they be expected to do so. They are not usually interested in how you dot your i's or cross your t's, but are interested in being able to tell the difference between an "i" and a "t." Teachers want, need, and expect neat, readable papers, and a sloppy, unreadable mess is grounds for a poor grade.

A typewriter is best for long writing assignments. Learning to type will be one of the most useful things you can do. This skill comes in handy in situations outside of school as well as in. If your school or community center doesn't offer typing classes, then you can buy (or borrow from a library) a self-teaching typing book that comes with records or tapes to guide you. If you can't afford to buy a typewriter of your own (and many second-hand shops and *Penny Saver* newspapers advertise great buys on used ones), then see if you can borrow one from a friend or arrange to use one in school during off-hours.

A typewritten paper won't guarantee an A+ paper, but it will be a welcome sight to the sore eyes of an English teacher who has graded 30 papers and comes upon a neat, easy-to-read 31st.

6. Apply for a library card. One of the best things in life is really free. In most communities, a library card is yours for the asking (with proper identification), so why not take advantage of the opportunity to own one? Library facilities range from books and periodicals to microfilm, records, tapes, and photographs, and can help you with almost any type of school assignment, in addition to providing an atmosphere conducive to studying.

Make it your business to get personally acquainted with your school or local library facilities and with the staff who maintains them. It will be much more fun to wander around the library and learn what it has to offer when you have some free time, rather than when you are working frantically under the pressure of an assignment.

7. Read, read, read . . . Reading what others have written is one way of increasing your vocabulary and seeing how professional writers use words to clearly express ideas. Read everything — newspapers, magazines, books, journals, billboards, boxtops, and bumper stickers. If you run into a word that you don't know, look it up in a dictionary and commit it to memory or use it in a sentence. If in your reading you train yourself to become aware of what is considered to be good writing, you will be amazed at how easy it will be to recognize bad writing — yours or anyone else's.

8. Keep a journal. Why wait for a specific writing assignment from your teacher to inspire you? Why not keep a notebook or pad of paper handy for ideas that come to mind every or every other day? Try to make it a habit to write for five or ten minutes a day on anything that comes to mind. This journal doesn't have to be like a private diary — it can merely be an organized place to record bits and pieces of ideas that may prove helpful on a future theme or report. Things such as jokes, observations, questions, quotations, anecdotes, new words, favorite poems, snatches of memorable (or even overheard) conversations, ideas for stories, news items, and character sketches are all journal material. If you do start a journal, don't feel that you must write in it every night. Let it be something you look forward to doing for fun, and don't let it become a chore.

Give journal-writing a try. And to show you how easy it is to get started, there's a journal just waiting for words on page 120.

9. Brainstorm. Sometimes you need to talk to other people about ideas that are brewing in your head. Brainstorming with a group of friends before beginning a writing assignment can be a creative and rewarding experience. Getting together with a small group of friends is a good way to get feedback on some of your ideas and a great place to give and get *constructive* criticism. If two or three of you come up with similar ideas for a paper, then work it out to write the paper from two or three different angles.

10. Buy a dictionary and a thesaurus. Two of the most useful books a writer can own are a dictionary and a *thesaurus*. (Look up the proper pronunciation in any dictionary!) You don't have to keep one under each arm as you write, but it is advisable to keep them both nearby.

If you are a bad speller it doesn't have to affect your grade — if you play it smart. One of the major advantages of a dictionary is that all the words in it are spelled correctly. So, when in doubt, look it up. (Many professional writers have admitted to having spelling problems, so be assured that you are not alone.)

If you have used the adjective "wonderful" ten times in one paragraph, you are greatly in need of a thesaurus. This handy reference book will provide you with interesting substitutes or synonyms that you can use in place of the over-used "wonderful," or any other old stand-by word that could use a rest.

Here are the titles of a few good, low-cost paperback editions of these valuable books. (Or ask your teacher for the names of ones she or he might recommend.)

> *American Heritage Dictionary*
> *The Random House Dictionary*
> *Webster's New World Dictionary*
> *Roget's Pocket Thesaurus*
> *Dictionary of Synonyms*
>   *and Antonyms* (Popular Library)

UNDERSTANDING THE ASSIGNMENT

It's a mistake to walk out of a classroom without completely understanding the assignment that your teacher gave you. Too often a D or an F paper staring back at a stunned student is because she or he misunderstood exactly what was expected. Yes, it's the teacher's responsibility to thoroughly explain an assignment, but it's *your* responsibility to come up with any questions that, when answered, will clear up any confusion you might have.

When it comes to asking questions, remember these tips:

1. Don't *ever* avoid asking a question for fear you'll sound stupid. Most likely, if you are confused, everyone else is as well and will silently thank you for speaking up. If shyness is a problem, however, wait until after class is dismissed and ask the teacher your question privately.

2. Don't sit and wait for someone else to ask a question that you'd like answered. You might be waiting a long, long time. And just because someone doesn't ask the question you have in mind doesn't mean that it's trivial or unimportant. *Anything that you don't understand is important.*

3. Don't expect your teacher to be a mind reader and know what you would like further explained. She or he may have a hard time "reading" the looks of over 30 faces, and it's just possible you may look like you really do understand something when, in fact, you're in a fog.

4. Before you leave the class make certain that you know the answers to these basic questions:
   1. What is the purpose of the assignment?
   2. What *exactly* am I to do?
   3. Must I type my paper or can it be handwritten?
   4. How long should the paper be?
   5. When is the paper due?
   6. What is the penalty for a late paper? (This knowledge should keep you on time!)

HUNTING DOWN GOOD IDEAS

What to write about is often the chief problem faced by many students when they receive an assignment. Sometimes a teacher will offer broad topics as possible ideas, but even then it is still up to the student to go from the general to the specific.

What should you do when your teacher ends class with: ". . . and you may write on any topic of your choice"? How does a person go about getting ideas? Try the following routes beginning with . . .

1. **Don't panic!**
2. **Use your own experience.** Luckily (or hopefully) you haven't spent your life in a soundproof booth with no windows, doors, or any contact with the outside world whatsoever. Living in such a situation would be about the only acceptable excuse for not having anything to write about — except, perhaps, "Life in a Soundproof Booth."

It is vital to your writing that you learn to observe the world around you with a fresh, alert eye. Look at familiar scenes with the awareness of seeing them for the first time. Try to train your eyes to act as a camera and your ears to act as a tape recorder. As you practice this you will soon become skilled at "photographing" and "recording" meaningful impressions in your mind. When an assignment rolls around you can draw on your memory of these experiences or, if you've started a journal to store a written record, you can get an interesting idea as effortlessly as rereading your notes.

If you are now saying, "Well, that's a good idea for people who travel a lot, have a lot of free time, or extra money to do really *exciting* things," you are trapping yourself in what has come to be known as the but-nothing-interesting-ever-happens-to-*me* excuse. Give yourself more credit than that! Even simple, everyday activities can make interesting papers if you work at it. How about a serious essay on the advantages and/or disadvantages of school cafeteria food? Or a humorous piece on the "art" of cleaning your room? Or bathing a dog? Or making a salad? Creativity has no set rules and no limits (except, perhaps, those set by your particular teacher). So, if you can make brushing your teeth sound interesting, then do it.

3. Use other people's experiences. Listening and talking to other people is something you do all the time. But this type of interaction has become so automatic in some of us that potential writing ideas probably just fly by. Around the time of an assignment, why not make a special effort to pay attention to the people around you and what they have to say? Talk to fellow students, your parents, your teachers, your friends, and anyone else you can strike up a conversation with. Talk to them about a particular assignment. Exchange views. Perhaps they can offer valuable insight or interesting topic ideas. You don't have to be formal about these discussions, but you might want to ask a specific question you have in mind. You'll probably be surprised with the way other people can provide such inspiration.

Information that comes from other people is worth taking the time to investigate. Treat it like a recipe being passed along from cook to cook. Add a drop of this or take out a pinch of that, and feel free to substitute various ingredients, turning the recipe into your own prize-winning dish.

4. Read newspapers and magazines. One of the best sources of food for thought is the printed word. And those of you who want to stay on top of *all* your classes should make it a habit to keep up on the latest events through reading (and *not* just by watching TV!). Even if you are not ordinarily interested in news stories, make it a habit to at least scan these various publications for composition ideas. You'll find that current events is just one of the hundreds of subjects you'll find in print. Everything from beauty tips and health reports to movie star gossip and film reviews is written up somewhere. There is probably no subject so odd that there is nothing written about it.

If you have no access to a variety of magazines or newspapers, go to your neighborhood or school library. There you'll be able to find thousands of ideas literally at your fingertips. Browse around for a while and if you find an interesting article or news item that you want to investigate more thoroughly, you can look in the subject-card catalog or in the *Readers' Guide to Periodical Literature* for more specific information.

P.S. While you're there, don't forget to apply for your own library card. Remember that it's free and will certainly come in handy.

5. Use TV, radio, and films as inspiration. While you're letting the different media entertain you, let them help you with your schoolwork as well. You can do this by simply thinking while you're watching and/or listening. Analyze one of the characters in your favorite situation comedy. Do further research on the topic presented on *60 Minutes* or *Good Morning America*. Use a dramatic storyline as a springboard to an original essay. Does the type of gadgetry used in James Bond films really exist? Find out. Discuss how the horror or science-fiction movies of today compare with those filmed 30 years ago. Is there a story in that latest number-one hit song? Why would anyone want to be a disc jockey?

These are only a tiny fraction of the types of composition ideas that can spring from your everyday contact with the media. Learn to turn an ordinary activity into a rewarding and interesting experience.

If you are still complaining that you can't think of a single thing to write about, you are simply blinding yourself to the ideas that are all around you. The trick is to recognize them for what they are. Don't be afraid to reach out and try something new or make something new out of something old. Surprise your teacher and yourself with a topic to replace "My Summer Vacation" or "My Favorite Person."

NARROWING THE TOPIC

Once you've decided upon a topic for your composition you have to concentrate on narrowing it down to a controllable size. By doing this you will save yourself time, extra work, and most of all, frustration.

Papers dealing with "A History of Dancing," "Crime Prevention," or "Sports Heroes" are good topics but not A+ material because they are far too broad to be adequately covered in one paper. First of all, a complete history of dancing could take you years to thoroughly research. In the second instance, you could write an entire book on crime prevention and still overlook many aspects of the subject. And, finally, you could write a twenty-page paper about *baseball's* heroes alone without even touching on the heroes of all the other sports that exist.

Learn to break your topic down. If dancing interests you, why not develop a paper about one particular aspect of dancing — ballet, tap, or disco. Better yet, why not an essay about the influence one of these dance forms had on the clothing or film industry. Crime prevention can be broken into subheadings emphasizing different aspects of the topic, such as helping teenagers go straight or training the elderly in self-defense. The subject of sports heroes can be personalized to include your favorite sportspersons or turned into a report on the huge salaries today's sports stars demand. Whatever the assignment, with a little more thought, each of these three subjects can be trimmed and adapted to fit the bill.

Here are two tips about narrowing your topic:

1. Choose a topic that is both interesting and practical. Don't begin writing about something that has the danger of becoming boring to you after just a few hours of working on it. Also, try to choose a topic that you know something about or can research in a reasonable amount of time. In other words, know your limits regarding interest and time.

2. Don't try to do the impossible. Many of the subjects that students decide to tackle cannot be adequately covered in a full-length book! Focus your topic so that it can be intelligently discussed in the number of pages you are aiming for. If your teacher doesn't give you a minimum or maximum number of words or pages, give yourself a rough estimate or goal. Be realistic and take into consideration the time allotment and subject material. Certainly your writing will benefit.

DEVELOPING A THESIS

Once you've cut your chosen subject down to a controllable size, it's still not time to start writing until you decide what direction your paper is going to take. What is it you would like to say about this topic? You can't go into everything you know about it — that would be both dull and time-consuming.

For example, suppose you decide on the general subject of *food* and reduce it in size as follows: *food — fast food — fast-food chains*. Well, what *about* fast-food chains? Before you begin writing you must take one more step and convert the subject into *an idea about the subject*. For example: *"Fast-food chains offer nutritious meals at convenient, low prices."* This statement or point of view toward the subject is called the "thesis." It will provide a guideline for what you should and should not include in your paper.

The thesis of your paper should state what the topic is and show your intention. Its purpose is to keep both you and your reader on the track by helping you to organize your material and your reader to follow your train of thought — knowing in what direction you're taking him.

Here are five points to remember when developing a statement of purpose or a "thesis" sentence:

1. Write a complete declarative sentence that reflects your point of view. Don't write your thesis in the form of a question, phrase, or word.

2. Write a thesis sentence that is somewhat open to argument, rather than a self-evident fact (e.g., "Fast-food chains offer nutritious meals at convenient, low prices" [somewhat open to argument], rather than, "Many people eat at fast-food chains" [known fact]).

3. Write a thesis sentence that is somewhat open to argument, rather than a simple statement of personal preference or observation with which no one can disagree (e.g., "Any teenager who's ever been in love will enjoy *Romeo*

and Juliet'' [somewhat open to argument], rather than, ''I loved the play *Romeo and Juliet''* [simple statement of personal preference]).

4. Write a thesis statement that is limited in scope, one that covers only what you want to discuss in your composition. For example, the thesis ''Fish make terrific pets'' is too broad. Will you really discuss *all* types of fish? *All* ways that they make good pets? Probably not. A better thesis would be: ''Goldfish are terrific, easy-to-care-for pets.'' This more limited thesis lets your reader know she or he will be reading about goldfish as easy-to-care-for pets.

5. Be creative. Sometimes it takes a little more thought and a little more time to come up with a new angle on your subject. But it'll be worth it. Not only will you have more fun writing about an interesting and original topic, but your teacher will enjoy reading a paper with a fresh, different outlook.

Here's a visual trick to help you learn how to narrow your subject down to a manageable size and to formulate a good thesis as the basis of your composition. Before you begin writing, think of your subject as a target. The outermost circle represents a very general subject — too broad to be handled in a well-formed paper; the next ring represents a slightly narrowed approach; and the next smaller ring represents a precise and limited topic. The innermost circle — the bull's eye — represents your point of view or ''thesis.''

16

Target Practice: From General Subject to Specific Thesis

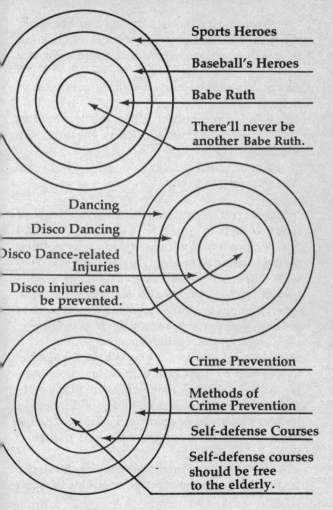

Sports Heroes

Baseball's Heroes

Babe Ruth

There'll never be another Babe Ruth.

Dancing

Disco Dancing

Disco Dance-related Injuries

Disco injuries can be prevented.

Crime Prevention

Methods of Crime Prevention

Self-defense Courses

Self-defense courses should be free to the elderly.

17

OUTLINES: RECIPES FOR SUCCESS

Following a recipe is a mystery to Sheryl X. Whenever she cooks something it is totally hit or miss. Oh, she does okay with tea and toast, but when it comes to something more exciting like a chocolate soufflé, Sheryl is definitely in need of help.

"Sheryl," one honest friend finally dared to say, "this chocolate soufflé is the absolute worst!"

"I know," Sheryl answered sadly. "But I just don't understand why."

Maybe you're familiar with a similar sense of failure when it comes to your writing. And maybe you, too, don't understand why nothing seems to come out right. Oh, you might do okay with simple sentences and very short paragraphs (like Sheryl manages with tea and toast), but when it comes to a longer, more involved piece of writing, you just can't seem to get it together.

Sheryl's trouble could have been avoided if she had used a recipe. It would have helped her to see, step-by-step, how to make an edible soufflé. And don't think that recipes are just for beginners either. Experienced and confident cooks let recipes be a basic guide and adapt or change them to suit their (or their guests') particular tastes.

Any trouble you might have with writing can be avoided by a kind of recipe or outline that you create for yourself. An outline should list, in a logical and orderly manner, everything that you want or need to include in your paper. You'll probably find that a good outline will help you get facts and ideas straight before you begin to write. And, whether you type your outline formally on a piece of typing paper, or scrawl it informally on the inside of a gum wrapper, an outline will give you a sense of order and keep your next composition from being a hit-or-miss experience.

OUTLINE WARM-UPS: LISTING AND CATEGORIZING YOUR IDEAS

The first step toward creating a workable outline is to *list all your ideas related to the thesis of the paper*. At this point you shouldn't worry about the order of your ideas or whether you will even use them all in your final paper. Just force yourself to jot down everything you know or think you can use in a paper on your chosen topic. (For some reports this list may include some information you've gotten by doing some research.)

Here's an example of what a list of ideas (or composition "ingredients") might look like if you were going to write a paper on the topic of "Education," with your thesis being, "Getting a high school diploma is the most important thing you can do."

1. get a better job
2. make more money
3. have greater self-confidence
4. gain respect from others
5. improve basic reading, writing, and math skills
6. make good friendships
7. win confidence of others
8. impress family and friends
9. get invited to the senior prom
10. qualify for college
11. learn to accept greater responsibility

Notice that there is no order to this list. The items are simply ideas that might occur in your head as you think about the thesis statement. In this case, the ideas are all reasons explaining "why?" (If you were comparing two things, such as high school graduates and non-graduates, you would have two lists of ideas.)

Once you have thought through all the possible ideas related to your thesis and listed them on paper, the next step is to order or *organize* them into a useful outline from which you can begin writing. In order to do this you must first group your ideas into common categories and eliminate any ideas that don't fit into your plan, either because they are unrelated to the subject or, if included, would make the composition too long. For example, in going over this list, you might decide to eliminate #6 and #9 because they both are related to the social aspects of high school that you decide not to discuss. This leaves you with nine items remaining that could be grouped as follows: Items 1, 2, and 11 all deal with job benefits. Items 3, 4, 7, and 8 all deal with character and personality benefits. Items 5 and 10 deal with academic benefits. Basically, this grouping is an outline. All you need now is the proper form.

SUITABLE ARRANGEMENTS: PUTTING YOUR OUTLINE IN ORDER

Once you've identified categories for your items and eliminated the unwanted ideas, you need to choose a logical arrangement for your reasons, facts, or examples. Here are some of the numerous methods of arrangement you may choose from:

1. Chronological (time) order
2. Order of importance
3. Spatial order (from place to place, near to far, left to right)
4. Comparison and contrast
5. General to specific

The order thought to be most effective for this sample outline consisting of reasons supporting the thesis statement ("Getting a high school diploma is the most important thing you can do") is *order of importance*. The decision, of course, is up to each individual writer. What must be considered is fulfilling your purpose and satisfying your reader at the same time.

OUTLINES: COMPACT AND MID-SIZE MODELS

The Topic Outline

Probably the easiest and clearest outline to make and understand is the topic outline. Each item listed is simply a topic to be discussed in the paper and is *not* a sentence. For most of the outlining you will do for school assignments, the topic outline should be quite adequate unless your teacher prefers a more detailed plan such as a sentence outline provides.

The Sentence Outline

A sentence outline uses what its name implies — complete sentences. It is always clearer than the topic outline because it gives more details about the meaning of each topic mentioned. If you have a poor memory, you might find a sentence outline more desirable.

Here is a comparison of the topic outline with the sentence outline. Study the form and detail of each, noting that every main heading must have at least two subheadings. Adapt whichever you are more comfortable with when it's time to outline your own paper, keeping in mind that they are both correct and acceptable (unless your teacher specifies otherwise).

Topic Outline
I. Personal Benefits
    A. Greater self-confidence
    B. Respect and confidence from others
    C. Impress family and friends
II. Academic Benefits
    A. Improve basic skills
    B. Qualify for college
III. Career Benefits
    A. Better job
    B. More money
    C. Greater responsibility

Sentence Outline
I. A high school diploma provides personal benefits.
    A. A person gains greater self-confidence.
    B. A person gains respect and confidence from others.
    C. A person impresses his/her family and friends.
II. A high school diploma provides academic benefits.
    A. It improves basic skills, such as reading, writing, and math.
    B. It may qualify you for college.
III. A high school diploma provides career benefits.
    A. It can help you get a better job.
    B. It can help you make more money.
    C. It can qualify you for greater responsibility.

WHAT'S IN A NAME? CHOOSING A GOOD TITLE

Once you've chosen a topic, narrowed it down, developed a thesis, and produced some sort of outline, you should take the time to think of a working title (it can be changed later if you come up with one that's more interesting — that's why it's called a "working" title). Many students find that thinking of a good title *before* beginning to write is inspirational. For one thing, it provides a sense of accomplishment and, for another, a good title can give you direction and help to bring your subject into sharper focus.

Although a terrific title cannot magically turn a frog of a paper into a prince, there is no reason to settle for less than your creative best. The title is, after all, the first thing your readers see, and you want to arouse their interest, not lull them to sleep.

Think of how boring life would be with meals consisting only of bread and water and you'll have some idea of how your teacher feels sitting down to read a pile of compositions all with titles like, "Book Report," "Summer Vacation," and "I Hate Television." These titles, like a diet of bread and water, are adequate, but very, very dull. It's hard to stifle a yawn before reading even one word.

Why not put your imagination to work and attract readers with titles that are flavorful and different. Rather than a (yawn!) title like "Dieting" for an essay on coping with the frustrations of losing weight, you could call your paper, "Don't Be a Sore Loser." A composition about your summer job as a lifeguard could be titled, "Sitting Pretty" instead of (yawn!) "My Summer Job."

Titles frequently fall into three different categories. It's your decision as the writer to choose the one that suits your purpose.

- **Summary titles** are those that provide the most general information. By giving facts without details they lure the reader into the paper if she or he would like to know more. Newspaper headlines are frequently good examples of these kinds of titles: "Hurricane Hits Florida Coast," "Sunset Concert Series Starts Saturday," and *"Star Wars* Breaks Box Office Records."

- **Preview or Give-a-Glimpse titles** aim to create reader curiosity. They introduce the subject by attempting to grab a reader's attention with a question or thought-provoking statement like "If Shakespeare Were Alive Today," "Why Won't Disco Disappear?" or "Where Will You Be in 2001?"

- **Teasing or Whimsical titles** leave your reader guessing about what's to come. They usually refer to the subject indirectly and make readers curious enough to read on. These titles can be fun for both the writer and the reader, although you might want to include a subtitle under the teaser to avoid any confusion. How about something like "Good Morning, Sunshine" (subtitled

"Solar Energy in Our Town") or "Boiling Water and Opening Cans" (subtitled "My Turn to Cook").

A striking title, whatever the type, can only work in your favor. Just be certain that it is not misleading. A good title should *honestly* lure the reader into the rest of the paper and not promise more than it will actually deliver. (Several newspapers and magazines are noted for sensational-type headlines. This practice of selling a product by exaggerating what's in the copy only serves to anger and alienate readers and is *not* a recommended example to follow.) Here are some things to keep in mind when you're trying to think of a good title:

1. Consider the material. The title should be related to the central idea or thesis of your paper.

2. Consider the audience. Will your readers understand a serious, technical title? Will they appreciate a humorous or clever title?

3. Consider the wording. Pick your words carefully, thinking of how they sound as well as what they mean. (Rhyming, alliteration, and onomatopoeia can prove interesting if used cleverly.)

Chapter 2

THE WRITE TIME: Getting Together the Rough Draft

IT'S ABOUT TIME

It's important to leave yourself enough time before the due date to be able to write at least one rough draft. (In fact, many professional writers admit to writing six or seven drafts of something until it pleases them!) If there's one thing A+ compositions probably have in common, it's that they are all products of at least one revision. To do this, and to do it well, you must arrange your time wisely. You need to be able to dash off your rough draft, then put it aside for a while. You need time to get away from it so that when you are face-to-face with it again, you can look at it freshly, with the enthusiasm that you may have lost had you been locked up together for too long a time. Sometimes writing that looked bad yesterday looks much better today. Arrange your time so that pressure doesn't force you to hand in something less than your best.

STARTING IS HALF THE BATTLE

If you have trouble getting started writing, you are normal. But it is a known fact that when the first word is written, you're on your way. So, sharpen your pencils or change the typewriter ribbon, feed the dog, dry the dishes, and get going! Simply sit, with your outline in front of you, and type or scribble the first words that come into your head.

The trick is to write your first draft as fast as possible. Resist the temptation to stop and revise after every few lines or paragraphs. Don't worry at this point about details like spelling, punctuation, or even sentence structure. If, while you're writing, you can't think of a particular word, leave a blank and fill it in later. Your purpose is to get your thoughts down on paper in a fairly organized manner that will be polished up on your second (or even third) time around. (Just be sure to leave extra-wide margins and lots of space between lines so you'll have room to revise on the same paper.)

As you're writing your first draft, remember that your outline was not chiseled in stone. If you find as you go along that it needs to be rearranged — do it. Many writers find that once they start writing they must reorganize as the paper proceeds. But having an outline in the first place gives you a place to start and helps to save time and frustration.

SOLID FOUNDATIONS: THE BASICS OF PARAGRAPHING

Don't be nervous about writing a good composition because if you can write a good paragraph, you're more than halfway there. A single paragraph is like a mini-composition. And, a good single paragraph is planned as thoroughly as a good composition. It has a single controlling idea, it uses a variety of details to develop that idea, and it ties all the ideas together into one logical group of sentences. Each group of sentences (the paragraph) should work together to advance the overall theme of the paper.

If paragraphs didn't exist, it wouldn't take a reader too long to get tired of looking at an entire page of writing that goes on and on without a break. You need to guide the reader along with signs of where you are going with your thinking. Paragraphs provide these signs and indicate to a reader where one idea leaves off and another begins. Obviously, good paragraphs don't just happen — they're created. Here's more on how.

Topic Sentences

The sentence which presents the topic to be

discussed within the paragraph is called the topic sentence. Every other sentence in the paragraph should be closely related to this topic sentence.

Many writers place their topic sentence at or near the beginning of the paragraph. A topic sentence near the beginning helps both you and your reader by clearly stating the main point of the paper before going on to develop it. However, in a long composition, it would be boring and monotonous to have the topic sentence at the beginning of every paragraph. So, it's a good practice to alternate the position of your topic sentence. For a change of pace, try it in the middle or at the end of the paragraph. As long as you use good supporting sentences to develop the topic sentence, feel free to move it where you think it will be most effective.

Here are some "shapes" your paragraphs might take depending on where you place the all-important topic sentence:

The Funnel Paragraph
Topic Sentence at the Beginning

Although I know there's a gimmick behind every trick, magic will never fail to amaze me. Yesterday, as my parents and I watched closely, my brother made a coin disappear. I suspect that it wasn't an ordinary coin, but when he let me look it over it appeared very real. Perhaps I'll check out a book on Houdini and learn how to make my brother disappear!

The Diamond Paragraph
Topic Sentence in the Middle

Yesterday, as
my parents and I
watched closely, my brother
made a coin disappear. I suspect
that it wasn't an ordinary coin but when
he let me look it over it appeared very real.
**Although I know there's a gimmick behind every
trick, magic will never fail to amaze me.**
Perhaps I'll check out a book on Houdini
and learn how to make my brother
disappear!

The Pyramid Paragraph
Topic Sentence at the End

Yesterday, as
my parents and I
watched closely, my
brother made a coin disappear.
I suspect that it wasn't an ordinary
coin, but when he let me look it over it
appeared very real. Perhaps I'll check out a book
on Houdini and learn how to make my brother disap-
pear! **Although I know there's a gimmick behind every trick,
magic will never fail to amaze me.**

31

Developing Topic Sentences into Paragraphs

Once you've written a topic sentence you usually can't let it stand alone. What you need now is a group of sentences that will support the idea expressed in your topic sentence. Here are six main ways you can build evidence to support your topic sentence:

1. with facts
2. with examples
3. with an incident or anecdote
4. with reasons
5. with comparisons or contrasts
6. with definitions

The support sentences that you create may be any one (or a combination) of the above methods. The important thing is to fully and effectively develop the topic sentence. If you give it little or no support, your entire paragraph will be weakened.

Here's the list again. But this time each method is accompanied by an example. Study these methods and keep them in mind whenever you begin writing.

1. A paragraph may be developed with facts. Supporting your topic sentence with factual information may make what you are saying more believable. Just make certain that you are distinguishing between fact and opinion. A fact is something that can be demonstrated to be true. An opinion, no matter how expert, is not neces-

32

sarily based on fact.

This year's homecoming weekend proved to be the costliest in Glenbrook High's history. The athletic department bought new uniforms for the football team at a cost of over four hundred dollars. The "Welcome Back" brunch, sponsored by the senior class, served 150 alumni for a grand total of two hundred dollars. And, the junior class, anxious to put on a dance worth remembering, spent one hundred dollars on decorations alone.

2. A paragraph may be developed with examples. Good examples can help to illustrate a topic that deals with something abstract (like beauty, truth, or freedom) because they give your reader something concrete to relate to.

Jenny is one of the nicest people I've ever met. For instance, if you're out of school just one day, Jenny is the type of friend who is first to call and find out what's wrong. She's also the kind of person to lend a helping hand, whether it's with homework, babysitting, or even washing the dishes. Another thing about Jenny is that she always has time to listen to her friends. I think her middle initial, "C," stands for "Consideration."

3. A paragraph may be developed with an incident or anecdote. Telling a brief story can be an interesting way of supporting the idea in your topic sentence. Of course, an incident or anecdote is a particular type of example. But they are examples with a story behind them. Just make sure that the story you tell is clearly related to the idea expressed in the topic sentence.

Some people have to learn the hard way that cheating is a dangerous game. A friend of mine, who put off doing a research paper until the last minute, ended up handing in his older brother's B+ paper from five years before. When the paper was returned, it was marked with a red F at the top. "An F?" Glenn said to our teacher. "But I thought it was clearly at least a B+." "It was worth a B+," the teacher explained, "when your brother, Marc, first handed it in to me five years ago."

4. A paragraph may be developed with reasons. This is a good way to develop a paragraph whose topic sentence prompts a reader to immediately ask the question, "Why?" If you're trying to get a point across or give your side of an argument, try building a paragraph with logical reasons (that may themselves be supported by facts, examples, or incidents) that explain why you think and feel the way you do.

My parents just won't let me grow up. It seems that they watch over everything I do! They refuse to let me stay out after midnight — even on weekends! And, even though I have my driver's license, I can't take the car out alone. It's wonderful to be loved, but it's frustrating to be babied.

5. A paragraph may be developed with comparisons and contrasts. Sometimes you can clarify the idea expressed in the topic sentence by comparing or contrasting it with a similar, more familiar, idea.

A blind date can turn an ordinary Saturday night into a very special evening. Of course, accepting a blind date, like buying a lottery ticket, is taking a chance. But a lot of lottery tickets are winners, and the same is true of blind dates. Just don't get too easily discouraged; give yourself time to get to know the person. Remember that he or she took a chance, too!

6. A paragraph may be developed with definitions. When you really want to make your reader understand what you mean by a particular word or phrase contained in the topic sentence, and a short definition just won't do, you may want to devote a whole paragraph to the definition. This method may involve giving many facts and examples in order to make yourself clear.

Gorging yourself with "junk" food is the first sign you're on the road to ruin. Sugary, high-carbohydrate foods are high on calories and low on nourishment. A steady diet of cake, candy, cookies, soda pop, potato chips, pretzels, and ice cream will only make you fat, moody, and run-down. In short, they'll ruin your health.

IS THAT A FACT? SUPPORTING YOUR STATEMENTS

No one has to take your word for anything. Remember that truth as you write your first draft. No matter what type of paper you're writing, if you state something as a fact, be certain to include evidence that backs up your position. Not doing so will indicate that you did little or no research and could make your teacher think it was a last minute or lazy effort on your part.

Build a solid, thorough paper. If it's a report on the energy crisis, don't throw in a statement like, "More and more homes will soon convert to solar power," and let it go at that. Unless you qualify as a known energy specialist, no one is under any obligation to accept what you've said as true. Verify such a statement with a variety of facts quoted from newspapers, magazines, or television reports, and support the statement with quotes from architects, engineers, or government energy specialists. Do whatever you can to make your statements sound strong and full of authority.

Supporting a statement with facts does not mean, however, that you're not entitled to offer your opinion anywhere in the paper. Of course you can give an opinion about something as long as you make it clear that you are expressing your own view. In book and movie reviews, and some subject reports, your teacher will expect a personal opinion. Just remember to use the personal pronoun "I" in these instances where you are clearly speaking for yourself.

THE LONG AND THE SHORT OF IT: DETERMINING PARAGRAPH LENGTH

Generally, the length of a paragraph is determined by the topic sentence and the number of details that must be included to make the idea you are trying to get across clear and effective. However, even though there is no strict rule as to paragraph length, unless you're writing a personal letter or dialogue, anything much less than one hundred words is likely to be weak. Provide as much information as you can so that your paragraphs are adequately developed. (Two exceptions to this may be your introductory and concluding paragraphs, which are more for attention and emphasis and might benefit by being shorter than the developmental paragraphs.)

Looking at this from another direction, however, if your paragraph runs over three hundred words, you may be straying from the main idea. Be aware that you run the risk of confusing and/or losing a reader if your paragraphs are too long and include ideas not closely related to the topic sentence.

GOOD CONNECTIONS: MAKING SMOOTH TRANSITIONS

To be really good, your writing must be like a chain. The sentences and paragraphs must be linked together for strength and unity. Each sentence should have a connection to the one before it and, similarly, each paragraph should be a natural extension of the previous one. Making logical connections in your writing relies on good use of transitional words and phrases.

If you work at attaining smooth transition in your writing, your reports and compositions will be more understandable. It takes practice, but both you and your reader will be happier with a paper that really "hangs" together. Following are some specific ways to help you learn to make the right connections.

Pronouns As Linking Expressions

In order to keep the thoughts moving smoothly from sentence to sentence and paragraph to paragraph, use pronouns to refer to words or ideas in the preceding sentences or paragraphs. These pronouns will carry the reader back to what has just been said. They're sort of like built-in memory devices so you can be confident that your reader is following your train of thought.

The pronouns commonly used as linking expressions are *he, she, they, this, that, these, those, them,* and *it. This, that, these,* and *those,* when used as adjectives, also work as transitional devices.

Roller skating is an old-fashioned sport that has become an overnight sensation. *It* seems to be most popular with the disco crowds. *They* have changed their dancing shoes for roller skates and can be seen rolling to their favorite tunes at all hours of the day and night. Some may think *that* sounds a little crazy, but any roller-disco person will tell you, "*It's* just good, clean fun!"

You will probably understand *this* new fad much better if you actually try skating on your own. There are plenty of roller discos that rent skates to beginners. Just be sure to wear plenty of padding in case your sense of balance isn't what *it* used to be!

Connectives

Another kind of transitional device is a word or expression that connects what has preceded with what is to follow. These types of devices are called *connectives.* Use connectives to make your writing coherent. But be careful because too many of these words within one paper will make your writing seem awkward and artificial.

Here's a list of many commonly used connectives. Note that they are grouped according to their effect on your writing. Keep this in mind when you're about to use a connective, and choose one that would best suit your purpose.

CONNECTIVES USED TO INDICATE A TIME OR SPATIAL RELATIONSHIP:

soon, next, then, later, finally, eventually, first, second, (third, etc.), now, meanwhile, in the meantime, afterward, since, nearby, above, below, beyond, in front (in back), to the right (left).

CONNECTIVES USED TO INDICATE A SEQUENCE (TO ADD ANOTHER THOUGHT):

and, in addition, also, furthermore, moreover, another, likewise, similarly, next, finally, besides, again, first of all, secondly.

CONNECTIVES USED TO INDICATE CONTRAST:

but, on the other hand, however, rather, nevertheless, otherwise, yet, still, in spite of.

CONNECTIVES USED TO INDICATE RESULTS:

therefore, hence, because, thus, consequently, as a result, for, accordingly, so.

CONNECTIVES USED TO INDICATE EXAMPLES:

for instance, an example of this, for example, take the case of, in other words.

Big cars should be banned from the roads. *First of all,* they drink enormous amounts of fuel that is fast becoming scarce. *Secondly,* they poison the air with excessive exhaust fumes. *And, in addition to* both those things, they are demanding parking space that our cities just don't have the room to provide.

In spite of all the evidence against large-size cars, however, Detroit manufacturers still turn out a good number of them each year. They say there are still many orders for such vehicles, and, until the American people stop buying them, they will continue to be produced.

Repetition of a Key Word or Phrase

Help readers bridge the gap between paragraphs by repeating a key word or phrase from one paragraph in the first sentence of the next paragraph. Not only does this practice serve to carry thoughts from one part to the next, but it also acts as a means of emphasizing an important point.

Karen was upset over her misunderstanding with Lois. But she had thought it would blow over and everything would get back to the way it used to be. She never thought that the rumors would start. At least now she knew who her *real friends* were.

One of these *real friends* was Alison. Thank goodness she was one person who didn't listen to gossip. . . !

Direct References

Another way to keep your readers on track is by using direct references. You can refer directly back to a word or an idea used in preceding sentences and paragraphs by using synonyms (for a word) and summaries (of an idea).

Paul is a terrific guy who lives next door to us. He's always ready to lend a helping hand and you can tell that he really cares about the people who live in this part of town. When he rescued one of the little kids from a burning garage, *our neighbor* proved he was brave as well as kind.

Today, this *neighborhood "Superman"* will be honored by the town. It's wonderful how *that fourteen-year-old boy* can be such an inspiration to us all.

GRAND OPENINGS: CATCHING A READER'S INTEREST

The beginning of any paper is probably the most important part that you will write. It has the huge responsibility of presenting your thesis and making your purpose clear *and* of arousing the interest of the readers so they'll want to read further. One way to look at your introductory or opening paragraph is to compare it to bait that you're going to cast into a "sea" of potential readers. Here are some ideas on how to "hook" these readers from the very beginning:

The Plunge-Right-In Opener

Plunging right into your subject is a direct and very acceptable way of catching a reader's interest. But in using this approach, avoid at all cost such awkward statements as "This essay is about . . ." or "I am going to show that. . . ." Being direct and to the point is not a license to be boring. Bore your reader in line one and she or he may not be awake to learn that the rest of the paper is a winner!

Here are two plunge-right-in openers that aren't boring:

"New York has the dubious distinction of being closer than any other major city to a nuclear power plant."

—Nan Randall, "What if . . .?"
New York magazine, April 16, 1979.

"Journalists have been dismayed recently by a series of court decisions allowing searches of their news rooms, their notebooks and their phone records."

— David Gelman and Diane Camper,
"Probing a Newsman's Mind,"
Newsweek, April 30, 1979.

The Startling Statement Opener

A good, attention-getting opening paragraph includes a statement of fact or opinion that will intrigue or shock your reader. What you want to do is catch the reader by surprise and entice him to read further.

Here are some famous openings that may have already shocked or interested you:

"I don't think I'll ever get married."
— Judy Blume, *It's Not the End of the World*.

"I was sick — sick unto death with that long agony; and when they at length unbound me, and I was permitted to sit, I felt that my senses were leaving me."
— Edgar Allan Poe, "The Pit and the Pendulum."

The Question Opener

Asking a question at the beginning of your introductory paragraph is a good way to make it clear what your paper is all about. Your reader assumes that if she or he reads further, the question will be answered. (And, it is your responsibility to make certain it is answered!) It is also a good way to start because it forces the reader to think about the subject.

Are you familiar with these question openers?

"What can you say about a twenty-five-year-old girl who died?"
— Erich Segal, *Love Story*.

"How do we go about living a nourishing life?"
— Dr. Jerry Greenwald, *Be the Person You Were Meant to Be.*

The Story Opener

Everyone likes a good story and telling one at the beginning of a composition is an excellent way to attract your readers' attention. Just be absolutely positive that the story you tell is fairly brief and is related to the purpose of your paper. Because of an easy, informal style to storytelling, relating incidents or anecdotes can be as interesting to write as well as to read.

Here are the first few lines of some good story openers:

"The other night, a friend of mine sat down at the table and informed me that if I was going to write a column about women, I ought to deal straight off with the subject most important to women in all the world. 'What is that?' I asked. 'Beauty,' she said."
— Nora Ephron, "On Never Having Been a Prom Queen."

"One night, ten years ago, my father was complaining about his job. After 40 years of selling women's hats on the same street in Manhattan, the pay was still lousy, his boss didn't give a damn about him and nobody bought hats anymore . . ."
— Bernard Lefkowitz, "Life Without Work," *Newsweek*, May 14, 1979.

The Direct Quote Opener

Sometimes quoting someone else makes an unusual and interesting opening. The speaker may be an authority on your topic, the subject of your topic, or just someone (famous or not) who has made a pertinent comment about your topic. If you're writing a piece of fiction, it might be one of your characters who introduces the topic via a bit of dialogue. Some writers find that a "spoken" introduction adds importance or meaning.

How about these openers?

" 'Once you're successful, you can meet almost anybody in the world you want to meet,' says The Rolling Stones lead vocalist Mick Jagger."
— "Mick Jagger: On Rockin' and Rollin' and Running Around," *Celebrity* magazine,
September 1977.

" 'I had a couple of lean years,' says golfer John Mahaffey, 31. 'It takes a while to get everything back into shape.' "
— *People* magazine article on John Mahaffey, by Jim Calio, August 6, 1979.

As you can see by all of these examples, there's more than one way to catch a reader's interest. And, once you've got him on the line, don't let him get away!

Generally speaking, the length of your introduction should be directly related to the length of the entire essay. If your thesis can be supported with only three or four well-developed paragraphs, then one introductory paragraph will probably do the trick. But an essay with six or more major points (as you might have in some research papers) may require more than one paragraph to adequately introduce the topic.

One more thing about your introductory paragraph — don't include too much information. Your objective is to inform the reader just a little bit, but intrigue him a lot. Once you've hooked a reader, then you can load him up with information. But don't scare him away before you get the chance. Follow the method of newspapers the world over. They have a "lead" paragraph that includes the basics, "hooking" the reader from the start. Details can be revealed as your paper progresses.

MARVELOUS MIDDLES: KEEPING A READER'S INTEREST

Once you've created an opening that will "hook" your readers, you must get to the heart of the paper. Known as the "middle," the "body," or the "developmental paragraphs," this section is made up of what you have to say. It will be the longest part of the paper and will need careful organization. Here's where knowing how to develop a paragraph comes in handy!

A marvelous middle (and even the not-so-marvelous one) consists of a group of paragraphs (usually three to five paragraphs in an "average" length composition), with a structure similar to that of a single paragraph. Just as the topic sentence states the main idea of a single paragraph, your introduction states the main idea of your paper. And, similarly, as the main points of a paragraph are developed according to facts, examples, incidents, reasons, comparison and contrasts, and definitions, the main points of an entire paper are developed in the same ways. (Review the details of these methods of development in the first part of this chapter on page 32.)

It's a good idea to refer to your outline when concentrating on the middle of your paper. Hopefully you will have arranged the details according to a tentative plan. But if you haven't yet thought of a logical order for the details of your paper (or have changed your mind about what you'll include) reread the section, "Suitable Arrangements," in Chapter 1, page 21.

EXCEPTIONAL ENDINGS: CONCLUDING ON AN INTERESTING NOTE

A good piece of writing, like a good meal, leaves a person with a satisfying feeling. So, create your endings as carefully as you would a delectable dessert.

A whole paragraph of summary or conclusion may not be necessary. In a short paper, one or two concluding sentences are usually enough. But whatever the length, an ending should somehow remind the reader what it is you have said. It should summarize or reemphasize the major points of the composition or it may make a prediction about the future of the subject. And, since it's your last chance to get a point across, it may include a personal thought or opinion (just be sure you make it clear that it is an opinion and not a fact) or relevant quote.

A good ending will give the reader a sense of completion. But in creating one, stay away from endings with such phrasing as "And so I have shown that . . ." or "Now for my conclusion . . ." or "I hope you now realize that. . . ." A conclusion doesn't have to be labeled as such! If it's a good wrap-up of what was said, your readers will know what it is. Don't spoil your last contact with them by boring or insulting them. Keep it interesting to the end! They might even thank you for it.

Here are some exceptional endings that might prove interesting and inspirational:

"When all of this was done, a republic eventually came to pass but the sorrows, and the troubles have never left that tragic, lovely land. For you see, in Ireland there is no future, only the past happening over and over."

— Leon Uris, *Trinity*.

"And what I have called *The Amityville Horror* remains one of those dark mysteries that challenges our conventional accounting of what this world contains."

— Jay Anson, *The Amityville Horror*.

" 'We came into this world to work together, but we can't be Bee Gees forever.' Why stop now? Says Robin, 'We want to go out on top.' "

— Jim Jerome, "Hanging Out with the Bee Gees," *People* magazine, August 6, 1979.

Chapter 3

MATTERS OF STYLE: IMPROVING THE *WAY* YOU WRITE

Your style is the *way* you write as opposed to what you write about (the contents or message of your paper). Imagine two articles on the same subject. One writer produced an interesting paper while the other writer's paper was quite dull. How could something like that happen? The difference is probably in the *style* of their writing.

While there are no rights and wrongs regarding personal style, there are certain qualities that an interesting style does exhibit. By studying these qualities and learning to incorporate them into your own writing, you can turn out more interesting A+ papers in no time.

TONE TACTICS

In speech, hearing the tone of a person's voice helps you to understand fully the meaning of his or her words. For example, if a friend comes up to you after class and says, "I barely passed the English test," you can tell just by the tone of his voice (and perhaps the look on his face) whether he is surprised, happy, disappointed, or angered. Did he study hard and is disappointed at not getting an A? Is he surprised at doing so "well," considering he never cracked a book? Or is he happy because he crammed the last minute and just wanted a passing grade? Obviously, the words themselves convey only part of the meaning. It's the *tone* that gives words "personality" and emphasis, letting you know how a speaker feels.

Tone also exists in writing — it's the *sound* your writing makes. But, in this case, since the words are read and not heard, an author must communicate tone through word choice and sentence structure. Generally, there are two tones: the *objective* or impersonal (informative) tone; and the *subjective* or personal (emotional) tone.

An objective tone conveys information without showing anything about the writer's personal feeling or personality. It is most appropriate when you are writing expository essays, news articles, lab reports, and research papers.

The subjective personal tone also informs readers but mainly it communicates a writer's feeling or attitude about the subject. A subjective tone should be used when writing any kind of review, autobiography, or personal letters, as well as most persuasive and narrative essays.

Here are three things that you should consider before beginning to write any paper. Keeping them in mind will help you to create a tone that will produce the effect you want.

1. Think of your attitude toward your topic. What is your topic? How do you *feel* about this topic? What is your thesis? Is it something with which you agree or disagree? Are you sympathetic or detached? Are you amused or outraged? Be aware of your attitude so you can control whether or not it comes across in your writing. Some reports call for a formal, impersonal, detached manner, while some essays and book reports almost require that your attitude be clear to readers. Take a stand before you start.

2. Think of your purpose. What do you want to accomplish by writing this paper? Is it to present factual information? Is it to entertain? Is it to persuade readers, win them over to a cause you believe in? Is it to give your opinion of something? Is it to impress your teacher and get an A?

3. Think of your audience. Keep in mind who might be reading your paper. Your teacher? Your classmates? A group of nuclear scientists? A class of third graders? Once you've identified who you will be writing for, it is your responsibility to write in terms they will understand. This does not mean that you should change the facts or alter your beliefs in order to impress or interest your readers, but it does mean that you should use language that these particular readers will both understand and appreciate. After all, you don't *speak* to friends, parents, little children, teachers, doctors, or strangers with the same words or in the same voice. You'll find that the same practice holds true in writing.

When you are aware of your attitude, purpose, and audience, the right tone will almost occur automatically. But, most importantly, once you decide on a tone, be consistent. Abrupt changes can confuse a reader. If you start out in a subjective tone, stay in the subjective tone. There's nothing wrong with giving information along with your personal feelings as long as you don't suddenly switch to the more objective, impersonal voice. Give your paper one "personality" and be proud of it.

ON THE LEVEL: FORMAL, INFORMAL, AND COLLOQUIAL LANGUAGE

Most people choose to wear clothes that fit their mood as well as the occasion. Writers choose words for the same reasons. So, just as you might dress one way for a football game and another way for the junior prom, you might "dress" your writing one way for a book report and another way for a term paper.

The tone, or "personality," you want your paper to project will be established by the type of words and sentence structure you choose to use. Generally, your writing will fall into one of three categories or levels of English — Formal, Informal, or Colloquial (Non-Standard). Each level has its particular uses although there is crossover in some cases.

The chart below summarizes the three basic levels of language. Use it as a guide and *not* as a rulebook. Notice that most of your writing is, and should be, on an informal level. Some term papers may call for the technical language of a formal style and you might use slang in the dialogue of an informal, narrative essay. The important thing is always to use the language appropriate to the purpose of your composition.

LEVEL	CHARACTERISTICS	USES
FORMAL	Specialized or difficult vocabulary, relatively long sentences, few contractions, no slang, proper usage and punctuation, objective or serious tone.	Government and legal documents, medical reports, research papers, some textbooks, essays and articles for a *specialized* audience, serious speeches and lectures, some business letters and reports.
INFORMAL	Sentences of varying lengths, commonly used vocabulary (including idioms, slang, and contractions *where appropriate*), popular usage, personal *or* objective tone.	Newspapers, magazines, most textbooks, short school reports and essays, letters to friends and family, some business letters, political speeches.
COLLOQUIAL (Non-Standard)	Short, very simple sentences, grammatical errors, much slang, misspellings, limited vocabulary, localisms.	Dialogue intended to represent local dialects in books, plays, comics, movies, radio, and television.

SCINTILLATING SENTENCE STRUCTURES: HOW TO VARY YOUR SENTENCES

Your writing style will be more effective if you vary the length and structure of your sentences. Sentences having the same pattern and the same rhythm throughout your paper will produce a monotonous, choppy effect that could make your composition tiresome and boring to read.

If your paper is loaded with short sentences all starting with the subject, it's time for a change. Here are some suggestions on how to go from simple to compound and complex sentences and from the normal order of subject — predicate — complement, to other, more interesting arrangements.

1. Place the direct object of a verb before the subject.

Tears and anger I had expected, but total silence surprised me.

2. Begin your sentence with an adjective or with an adverb.

Wrinkled and leathery, the man's face was clearly a sign of old age.

Quietly entering the room, I took a seat in the back.

3. Open a sentence with a prepositional or a participial phrase.

Through the open window I could see the family eating their dinner.

Having known him all my life, I was convinced he was innocent.

4. For special effect, start a sentence with a coordinating conjunction, such as *and, or, nor* or *but.*

And, believe it or not, she lied!

But let me explain.

5. Try separating the subject and predicate by words or phrases.

The movie, *frightening and fast-paced,* was really terrific.

6. Occasionally, write a sentence that is a question or exclamation.

Isn't it time we helped the elderly in our neighborhood?

Volunteer, today!

7. Make a series of short, simple sentences into a longer, complex sentence.

Not this: Eric Lane is captain of North's football team. He showed up at Saturday's carnival alone. He and his girlfriend broke up.

But this: Eric Lane, captain of North's football team, showed up at Saturday's carnival alone because he and his girlfriend broke up.

8. Avoid long, "stringy" sentences that are put together by the overuse of the words *and* and *so.*

Use subordination of ideas (add clauses and/or

phrases) to replace and *and* so:

Not this: The temperature outside continues to fall *and* people's fear and anxiety grow, *and* this makes them nervous about not having enough fuel to heat their homes.

But this: As the temperature outside continues to fall, people's fear and anxiety grow, making them nervous about not having enough fuel to heat their homes.

Divide one sentence into two:

Not this: Ryan is a baseball fan *and so* he goes to every home game *and* he buys the best seats in the stadium *so* he can see better *and* maybe catch a foul ball.

But this: Being a baseball fan, Ryan goes to every home game. Since he buys the best seats in the stadium, he not only sees better, but is in a good position to catch a foul ball.

TAKE ACTION: USING ACTIVE VERBS

In writing, the difference between the active voice and the passive voice makes all the difference in the world. An active voice verb makes a sentence more direct and lively. A passive voice verb, however, is less forceful, and using a lot of them in one paper can produce awkward, less effective sentences.

The **active voice** of a verb shows who or what

59

is doing something — as in *Peter hit Matt* or *The wind pushed me down.* The **passive voice** shows who or what is being acted on — as in *Matt was hit by Peter* or *I was pushed by the wind.* As you can see from the examples, the active voice sentences are more concise and convey a more concrete picture than the sentences with passive verbs.

Although both the active voice and the passive voice are grammatically correct, active verbs are usually preferred. About the only instance a passive verb would be preferred would be when you want to emphasize the object of the sentence — by making it the subject. For instance, instead of *I will order the cake next week,* if you want to emphasize the *cake,* switch the sentence to read: *The cake will be ordered next week.*

TELL IT LIKE IT IS: THE ART OF BEING SPECIFIC

When you learn the "art" of using words to paint clear pictures of what you are saying, you'll be less likely to leave your reader pondering over blurred meanings. Words have color and texture just as paints do. And, to obtain the effect you want, you must choose the words as carefully as an artist would choose his color of paint.

For an A+ composition, use top-quality words to express your ideas. (But don't make the mistake of thinking that the best word is the one with more than seven syllables that fewer than five classmates know how to pronounce!) Memorize this rule: The best word to use is always the one that conveys the *exact* meaning you intend. The reader should never have to scratch his head, wondering what you are trying to say. Any abstract words (i.e., something which *cannot* be touched or seen: beauty, love, freedom, happiness) must translate into clear, exact meanings. Any concrete words (something that *can* be touched or seen: car, house, flower, food) must be made as specific as possible.

All words create mental images in a reader's mind, but these images are not necessarily the same in every reader. When you see the word "house," what do *you* think of? Your own house? Your best friend's house? A mansion? A shack? It all depends on your frame of reference. But a good writer can narrow down a reader's mental image of an abstract or non-specific word by being as descriptive as possible. Burt's house. A treehouse. The White House. An estate. A farmhouse. And, the more you narrow something down, the more concrete it becomes. Burt's giant, colonial house. A rickety, old treehouse, etc. The list of houses is endless, so if you have a particular one in mind, say so. If your words are too abstract, a reader will visualize what *he* wants to and may miss your point entirely.

"Food" is not at all specific; "hamburger, french fries, and a milk shake" are more specific. "Vehicle" is not at all specific; "car, bus, and motorcycle" are more specific. "Dog" is not at all specific; "French poodle, German shepherd, and fox terrier" are more specific. Too many abstract or non-specific concrete words in a paper will make your writing vague and underdeveloped. A reader needs enough specific concrete words to make the abstract clearer and more familiar.

Liven up your style and be as concrete as possible. Here are three good ways to do just that:

1. Illustrate abstract and non-specific concrete words with carefully chosen adjectives and adverbs.

(Note the words "carefully chosen." A sentence with seven mediocre adjectives and/or adverbs won't be as effective as a sentence with one or two *well-chosen* ones.)

Instead of: The guests were impressed by the food.

How about? The guests were impressed by an appetizing array of hot and cold food, elegantly served in the traditional Japanese style.

2. Illustrate abstract and non-specific concrete words with concrete examples.

Instead of: There were many delicious foods to eat at the picnic.

How about? There were platters of cheese and crackers; a huge buffet table covered with chicken, potato salad, cole slaw, and corn; wooden bowls overflowing with fruit; and mouthwatering strawberry shortcakes smothered with whipped cream.

3. Illustrate abstract and non-specific concrete words with similes and metaphors. *(Reminder: A* simile *is a direct comparison using the* *words "like" or "as." A* metaphor *is an implied comparison — it does not use "like" or "as.")*

Instead of: The guests ate a lot of food.
How about? The guests ate like vultures.

Instead of: The table had a lot of food on it.
How about? The table was a mountain of chicken and potato salad.

Help your readers to see, hear, feel, taste, and touch your words. Be specific. Be concrete. You'll be understood.

SHADES OF MEANING: RECOGNIZING THE CONNOTATIONS OF WORDS

Every word is made up of two parts, its *denotative* and its *connotative* meaning. The strict dictionary definition or basic meaning of a word is its *denotation*. For example, the word "tall" denotes "high in stature." Any pleasant or unpleasant associations, feelings, or suggested meanings of a word that go beyond its basic, denotative meaning are called *connotations*. Connotations of a word may be favorable or unfavorable depending upon each reader's specific personal reaction. Therefore, the word "tall" might connote "large" to one person, "graceful" to another, and "gawky" to a third.

Words that tend to have neither a favorable

nor an unfavorable connotation for most people are called *neutral words*. They may convey your meaning adequately, but do nothing toward giving the reader any specifics. Words such as street, liquid, restaurant, boat, drink, said, etc., are all examples of neutral words. These kinds of words will rely on surrounding words to give them more strength and meaning.

As a writer you can, of course, choose to write with only neutral words. But think how colorless and boring such writing would be! Instead, train yourself to be aware of the connotations of various words. When you want to express feelings that are favorable or unfavorable, try to select words that will have the right connotations for your purpose.

The examples below illustrate the range of positive and negative connotative meanings. Even though all three sentences in each set may share the same *basic* meaning, notice how the different connotations really contribute to the overall meaning.

Neutral: Brian *saves his money*.
Favorable: Daniel *is thrifty*.
Unfavorable: Andy *is cheap*.

Neutral: Gail is *short*.
Favorable: Lisa is *petite*.
Unfavorable: Alana is *shrimpy*.

Neutral: I rode in the *car*.
Favorable: Esther rode in the *limousine*.
Unfavorable: Charles rode in the *clunker*.

Neutral: Joyce ate in a *restaurant*.
Favorable: Richard ate in a *hotel dining room*.
Unfavorable: Steve ate in a *dive*.

Remember that the words you choose will influence your readers. Some words are "loaded" with connotation and must be used with care. Stuck in the wrong place they can change the whole tone and thus the whole meaning of your paper. After all, a *shrimpy* guy who drives a *clunker* and eats in a *dive* isn't necessarily *cheap*. Maybe he's just *thrifty*!

NOBODY SPEAKS "JARGONESE": AVOIDING CONFUSING WORDS

Most likely, your paper will not be put on a scale and assigned a grade according to its weight. So why load it down with a whole troop of meaningless words?

Jargon, from the French word meaning "babble" or "chatter," is the name given to language that uses big, vague, confusing words. A common characteristic of jargon is that it takes fifty words to say what could be said in ten. And, although nobody speaks "jargonese," millions are quick to put it into their writing.

Jargon is:

I regret to inform you that due to the fact you have canceled yet another date I must conclude our relationship.

When what the writer really means is:

Because you broke another date, we're through!

A paper filled with jargon may look impressive at first glance, but begin to read it and it won't really make sense. Pretentious and confusing, this kind of writing does nothing more than take up space and irritate a reader because he can't figure out what is being said. If a reader isn't sure about what a writer is trying to say, he or she can't reasonably judge the ideas and might take the easy way out by putting the paper aside and ignoring it. (Or, in a teacher's case, by giving it a poor grade.)

Why would a person purposely use jargon? Perhaps he or she is not clear on what to present in the paper. Inflated words tend to cover up poorly developed thoughts. But it's a thin disguise and sooner or later a reader will figure it out (probably sooner than later). If you're unsure of what to say in a paper or how to say it, take some time to think your ideas through before beginning to write. In the end, you'll save time, effort, and possible embarrassment. If you're at all confused about where you're going, how can you possibly lead anyone else there?

Another reason that some people use jargon is that they think it sounds impressive. But not many people are impressed by something that they don't understand. They just get frustrated and confused. Don't try to show off with jargon. It won't work. Be brief . . . and be yourself. Write with words that don't need a translation.

Here are two famous proverbs written in "jargonese." Can you translate them into plain English?

    A. It is advisable under most circumstances to restrain any impulses to numerically order one's poultry before the completion of incubation.

    B. In my opinion it would be unwise under the circumstances for those who inhabit glass dwellings to throw any geological specimens.

If it took you a while to figure out that A is, *Don't count your chickens before they're hatched* and B is, *People who live in glass houses shouldn't throw stones,* then think how long it would take you to understand an entire paper written in this language! Do yourself and your readers a favor and stick to plain talking.

SHORTCUTS: A GUIDE TO PLAIN TALKING

Learn to minimize jargon in your papers by remembering that it's word quality and not quantity that counts in writing. Eliminate phrases that just take up room in a sentence and replace them with simple, more direct words. Here are some space-saving suggestions:

INSTEAD OF	USE
along the lines of	*like*
by means of	*with, by*
despite the fact that	*though*
for the reason that	*since*
in the amount of	*for*
in the event that	*if*
in view of the fact that	*because*
it's my opinion that	*I think, I believe*
make an attempt to	*try to*
on the basis of	*by, from, etc.*
subsequent to	*after, following*
with respect (regard) to	*about*

Unless you're writing a formal research or term paper, avoid purely technical terms. *Don't use a word unless you know its exact meaning.* Of course it helps to use a thesaurus, but don't use it to write your whole paper and replace simple, right-to-the-point words with what you think are their more impressive equivalents. Why say "resides" when "lives" is so much clearer? Why bother with "deem" when "think" is available? And, why would you want to "ascertain" something when "learn" is so much easier? Get the idea? Don't go out of your way to try to sound impressive and be something you're not. Get the point across with words that work fast.

One last note: Beware of meaningless, repetitious words within a phrase. Do you really need the word "down" in the sentence: "He fell *down* from the tree"? (Very few, if any, people ever fall *up.*) What about the "out" in "Erase *out* all errors"? It's unnecessary! And why use the phrase "each and every" when the word "each" *or* the word "every" works very well alone. There's no prize for wordiness, so trim all phrases wherever possible.

AVOID CLICHÉS — LIKE THE PLAGUE!

A cliché (pronounced klē sha') is a trite expression that has been used so often by so many people that it has lost the freshness and originality it once had. Certainly the first person to have used the phrase "busy as a bee" must have been thought of as pretty clever. But after years and years of seeing "busy as a bee" in print and hearing it used in conversation, it is a dull, dull, dull addition to any piece of writing. A paper filled with a bunch of clichés may give your reader the impression that you are lazy and lack originality. Learn to use simple, straightforward language instead of worn-out phrases. Make your writing reflect how thoughtful and original you can be.

Since clichés come to mind so easily, you have to consciously watch out for them so they don't creep into your sentences. *Think* while you are writing and don't always opt for the easy way out. Be creative. Substitute new words for the old standbys.

Look over the following list of worn-out clichés. Use your imagination and revise each one of them. If you're ever tempted to use one of these tired, overused expressions, turn immediately to your original revisions.

REVISION

CLICHÉ	REVISION
After all is said and done	
Beyond a shadow of a doubt	
Break the ice	
Busy as a bee	
Cool as a cucumber	
Crystal clear	
Easier said than done	
Green with envy	
Heart of gold	
Last but not least	
To make a long story short	
Time flies	
White as a sheet	

BE CONSISTENT

Green traffic lights always mean "go." But what would happen if they meant "go" in your town and "stop" in the next? No doubt it would be dangerously confusing and probably cause a lot of accidents. Many drivers, stunned by the unexpected change, would become angry and frustrated. They might even give up driving! You see, a certain amount of consistency in everyday life is not boring, it's necessary. Consistency helps people feel secure when they're driving a car and, similarly, it helps them feel secure when they're reading.

How can consistency make readers feel secure? It keeps them from getting frustrated by letting them know what to expect. It lets them safely assume that some things in your paper will remain the same to the end. Following are some hints on how you can go about making your paper more consistent.

When you use names, abbreviations, initials, and numbers, make sure that you handle them the same way all through your paper. This means that you shouldn't use the full name Patricia on one page, and then, with no prior explanation, start using the nickname "Pat" on another. (It gets even more confusing if the nicknames are not just shortened versions of the originals, like switching from Richard to "Dick" or from Diane to "DeeDee.") You also can't refer to Dr. L. B. Hart on page one, and end your paper quoting him as "Leonard Hart." *You* might know that you are referring to the same person, but a reader may not make the connection.

Regarding abbreviations, a good rule to remember is not to use them except in certain instances where they are customary and therefore quite acceptable. (Acceptable abbreviations include: Mr., Mrs., Ms., Dr., Rev., St., A.D., B.C., A.M., P.M., i.e., e.g., etc.) In all other instances it is safest to spell everything out as it leaves little room for misunderstanding. If you stick to this rule, your paper shouldn't alternate between "California" and "CA" or between "France" and "FR." Don't test your reader's spelling ability. Spell it out for him.

Acronyms (words formed from the initial letter[s] of each of the successive parts [or major parts] of a longer term) are becoming more and more popular in the media. It's hard to pick up a newspaper without seeing such "words" as UNICEF, SALT, OPEC, and NASA. In addition to the acronyms there are the organizations that go by their initials even if they don't spell some sort of a pronounceable word. So we're surrounded by things like FDA, NBA, and CIA. Now if you have a terrific memory, coming upon these letters will never pose a problem. But if you are in the majority of those with not-so-great memories, you'd like a gentle reminder of what the letters stand for.

Don't ever assume that your readers have terrific memories. Make it a practice to write the name of the organization out in full when it's first mentioned in your paper. Place the acronym or initials in parentheses following the full word(s). Give your reader a chance to become familiar with the term and then later in the paper you can begin using the initials.

Consistency is the rule when it comes to your use of numbers, too. Spell out a number if it may be done in one or two words. All others should appear as numerals. For example, *1,300,275*, *$433.55*, and *1980* should appear as numerals, but *five*, *fifty cents*, and *sixty-one* should appear in words. (Of course, this does not apply to mathematical or scientific writing where most numbers are written as numerals and not spelled out.) And, never write a sentence that mixes both formats like, "Jason bought his Levis for $22.00 while I only paid fourteen dollars for mine."

ARE YOU GAME? PAINLESS VOCABULARY-BUILDING IDEAS

Believe it or not, a friendly game of *Boggle* or a heated contest on the *Scrabble* board can improve your writing style. Don't laugh at this notion, read on.

One of the biggest problems in writing any paper (after getting started, that is) is thinking of the right word at the right time. For some people word choice becomes such a slow, tedious process that their index fingers start to ache from turning so many pages in a dictionary or a thesaurus.

You can avoid some of the head, finger, and

stomach aches that writing is known to bring about if you learn to *consciously* build up your vocabulary. Searching for one specific word is so much easier if your supply of good words exceeds the demand. But keep in mind that words are not just in dictionaries — they're everywhere! Discover them in newspapers, magazines, books, pamphlets, billboards, labels, bumper stickers, boxtops, and, as mentioned above — games!

Games are a valuable means of building your vocabulary. And they're fun, too! *Scrabble, Word Power, Boggle, Words Worth, Spill 'n Spell, Probe,* and *Word Master Mind* are only some of the numerous vocabulary games out on the market today. All of them are good training for thinking of the right word at the right time — and fast. Start saving your allowance to chip in with family or friends to buy one or two of these interesting games. Prove to yourself (and others) that vocabulary-building can be a relaxing and entertaining experience.

If you make a real attempt to learn at least one new word a day, you'll be pleasantly surprised at the improvement in your writing. All it takes is effort. Now where have you heard that before?

Chapter 4

FINAL TOUCHES: EDITING, REWRITING, AND POLISHING

Congratulations! You've just written the first draft of your composition. Now you're all through, right? Wrong. Good, effective writing always involves rewriting no matter how terrific your outline is, no matter how many hours you've already spent working, no matter how smart you are, and no matter how neat your handwriting (or typing) is. *One draft just isn't enough.* Even the most professional writers have to edit, rewrite, and polish their work many times before they're satisfied with it. In fact, that's why they're known as professionals. They're thorough revisers and are rarely satisfied with a first (and sometimes even a second) draft. So, if the pros can benefit from rewriting, so can you. (The reproduction on page 77 shows page one of Sinclair Lewis's manuscript for his novel, *Babbitt*. Notice all the revisions!)

Editing and rewriting is your opportunity to iron out any of the "wrinkles" in your first draft. Of course there will be parts you don't feel need any changing, but it pays to be honest with yourself if you want to hand in the best possible paper. Would another word be better than the one you have? Are some of the sentences awkward and monotonous? Does a particular paragraph belong somewhere else in the piece? The better able you are to constructively criticize your own writing, the better the final product will be and, ultimately, the better your grade.

When you sit down to rewrite your paper, start by reading it aloud. This helps let you see your writing as your readers would see it. In fact, reading aloud is so helpful that you might want to do it several times as you work toward a finished piece.

The importance of revision as illustrated by Sinclair Lewis.

TRICKS OF THE TRADE

Careful editing and rewriting can be a slow and exacting process. So, here are some hints to help you get through it with a minimum of confusion:

1. Use a red pencil to edit. (Or any color that stands out from the color you used for the rough draft.)

2. If you discover you need to rearrange whole paragraphs (or add new ones), use a scissors to cut up the first draft and paste it back together in the order you want it. (Don't waste valuable time copying over parts you are satisfied with. Move things around and see your paper in its final new order before writing up the copy you'll hand in to your teacher.)

3. To rearrange sentences, simply draw a circle around those to be shifted and, using an arrow, show where they should be placed. If many sentences within a paragraph have to be rearranged, the circles and arrows might get too messy and confusing. In this case, *number* the sentences in the new order you want. Just make sure that when copying over the final draft you put these sentences in their new arrangement.

4. Use special proofreader's marks wherever possible. They'll save you time and make your second draft readable enough to be easily copied over into a final paper. Following is a list of the most common proofreader's marks and their meanings.

☰	(capital letter)	These three lines under a letter indicate that the letter should be capitalized.
/	(lower case or split letters or words)	This mark placed *through* a letter indicates that the letter should be lower case. Placed *between* two letters it indicates that two words should be formed.
∧	(caret insert)	This mark indicates that a word, phrase, or punctuation mark is being added.
ℛ	(deletion line)	This mark shows that a word, phrase, or punctuation mark is being taken out.
∾	(letter or word reversal)	This mark shows that two letters or two words should be reversed.
⌣	(connect)	This mark shows that two letters or two words should be joined together.
⁋	(paragraph mark)	This mark indicates the need to indent for a new paragraph.
⊙	(period)	This indicates that a period should be added.

Here's an example of proofreader's marks at work:

¶ Lucy r. Williams␂ a student at Ridgefaild High school, won the local spelling bee and will compete in the state finals on Saturday night at the Ridge field Holiday Inn. It will mean a lot to Lucy if her friends are there to cheer her to Victory. The Contest starts at 8 p.m. and admission is free.

YOU BE THE JUDGE: COMPOSITION CHECKLISTS

Presented below are two checklists that will help you smooth out your rough draft. When answering each question, try to be as honest as possible about your work. If in doubt about whether you should check "Yes" or "No," you might want to ask a friend to read your paper and give you *constructive* editorial comments.

1. After reading over your paper *once*, check off the items listed under "Organization and Style." *Anytime you check a "No" box, refer to the page number listed in parentheses to help you out.*

2. Reread your paper a *second* time checking for errors that relate to the "Grammar and Mechanics" section. *If you check a "No" box in this section, refer to your own grammar text or dictionary or to one of the lists at the end of this book (Spelling Demons, page 84; Punctuation Pointers, page 87).*

Organization and Style Checklist

1. My paper focuses on one specific topic. (page 13) Yes ☐ No ☐
2. I made my purpose clear from the very beginning. (page 14) Yes ☐ No ☐
3. Each paragraph presents one main idea related to the central topic. (page 19) Yes ☐ No ☐
4. The paragraphs are arranged in a logical order. (page 21) Yes ☐ No ☐
5. Each paragraph has a topic sentence (page 29) that is fully and effectively developed. (page 32) Yes ☐ No ☐
6. I have used transitions to link sentences and paragraphs. (page 38) Yes ☐ No ☐
7. I have written an attention-getting first paragraph. (page 42) Yes ☐ No ☐
8. I have written a clear conclusion. (page 48) Yes ☐ No ☐

9. I have used an appropriate tone. (pages 52 – 56)   Yes ☐   No ☐
10. I have varied the sentence patterns. (page 57)   Yes ☐   No ☐
11. I have used active verbs wherever possible. (page 59)   Yes ☐   No ☐
12. I have used specific, concrete words. (page 60)   Yes ☐   No ☐
13. I have said *exactly* what I mean. (page 63)   Yes ☐   No ☐
14. I have avoided jargon and tired clichés. (page 65-70)   Yes ☐   No ☐
15. My title reflects the point of my paper. (page 24)   Yes ☐   No ☐

Grammar and Mechanics Checklist

1. I have indented all paragraphs.   Yes ☐   No ☐
2. I have used only complete sentences.   Yes ☐   No ☐
3. All verbs are in the same tense throughout the paper.   Yes ☐   No ☐
4. Each sentence begins with a capital letter.   Yes ☐   No ☐
5. Each sentence ends with the proper punctuation mark. (page 87)   Yes ☐   No ☐
6. Every word is spelled correctly (see page 84 or a standard dictionary).   Yes ☐   No ☐

LAST-MINUTE MECHANICS

Most teachers will tell you how they want you to set up a paper for their particular class. But, if ever in doubt, here are some fairly universal guidelines for preparing the final copy:

1. When writing a paper by hand, use lined paper (of average spacing), 8½" x 11". Use blue or black ink, and *write neatly*.

2. If you type your paper, use 8½" x 11" white typing paper. Indent five spaces to begin new paragraphs, double space between lines of copy, and leave a 1½" margin on the left side of your paper, and a 1" margin on the right side.

3. Make certain that your name is on *all* pages of the final draft. (Preferably in the top right-hand corner.)

4. Do not number the first page of your paper (the title tells readers it's page one), but do number all subsequent pages. (Always use the numeral to indicate the page number, not the word.) Put the number beneath your name on each page.

5. Center your title at the top of your first page.

6. Proofread your final paper carefully. Don't be afraid to make changes with a pen if you notice mistakes. As long as your corrections are neatly made, your teacher probably won't consider it messy. Use common sense, though: If *you* can't read something, don't expect your teacher will be able to either.

SPELLING DEMONS

Certain words seem to stump even the best spellers over and over. One way to get over these trouble spots is to keep a record of words that repeatedly give you problems, putting special effort into memorizing them.

Fifty of the most commonly misspelled words are printed below. The next fifty lines are to be filled in by you. Record any words not already listed that tend to give you trouble (look up their correct spelling before writing them down). If it would be helpful to you, add a short definition following each word. Keep this personalized dictionary handy whenever you write and edit your compositions.

1. accommodation
2. adequate
3. a lot
4. athlete
5. bracelet
6. business
7. calendar
8. cemetery
9. competition
10. congratulations
11. definitely
12. embarrassment
13. exaggerate
14. familiarize
15. February
16. government
17. grammar
18. hospital
19. immediately
20. irresistible
21. leisurely
22. mediocre
23. mosquito
24. naive
25. occasion
26. occurrence
27. outrageous
28. pamphlet
29. pastime
30. permanent
31. pneumonia
32. privilege
33. procedure
34. professor
35. receive
36. recognize

37. recommend 42. similar 47. vacuum

38. rehearsal 43. souvenir 48. villain

39. restaurant 44. temperature 49. Wednesday

40. separate 45. truly 50. yacht

41. sergeant 46. twelfth

51. _____

52. _____

53. _____

54. _____

55. _____

56. _____

57. _____

58. _____

59. _____

60. _____

61. _____

62. _____

63. _____

64. _____

65. _____

66. _____

67. _____

68. _____

69. _____
70. _____
71. _____
72. _____
73. _____
74. _____
75. _____
76. _____
77. _____
78. _____
79. _____
80. _____
81. _____
82. _____
83. _____
84. _____
85. _____
86. _____
87. _____
88. _____
89. _____
90. _____
91. _____

92. _____

93. _____

94. _____

95. _____

96. _____

97. _____

98. _____

99. _____

100. _____

PUNCTUATION POINTERS

THE PERIOD (.)

1. Use a period after most declarative and imperative sentences.

Beatrice ate dinner at my house. (Declarative)
Please quit asking me my name. (Imperative)

2. Use a period after an indirect question or after a polite request.

Bill asked Cindy why she was late. (Indirect question)
Will you please lend me your sweater. (Polite request)

3. Use a period after standard abbreviations.
Ms., Mr., U.S.A., M.D., Jan., etc.

THE QUESTION MARK (?)

1. Use a question mark at the end of a direct question.

Is Ellen home?

2. Use a question mark after each part of a sentence containing multiple questions.

Are you going to visit London? Rome? Athens?

THE COMMA (,)

Since there are dozens of possible ways to use the comma, only the most important will be listed here. A comma's main purpose is to indicate natural pauses and breaks among written words. If when you proofread you make it a habit to read your paper aloud, you will be able to *hear* where most of the commas should exist.

1. Use a comma to set off appositives (words that clarify or identify that which precedes or comes before them).

Alan, my oldest brother, leaves for college on Monday.

2. Use a comma to set off a direct address (words that tell to whom a remark is directed).

Pay attention, Fran, so you don't make a mistake.

3. Use a comma after *yes* or *no* and after weak exclamations like *oh, why,* and *well.*

Yes, I'm going to the party.
Oh, I didn't know you were invited.

4. Use a comma to separate a direct quotation from the rest of the sentence.

"I want to go bowling," said Bruce.

5. Use a comma after each word in a series.
   I ate a hamburger, french fries, and a Coke for lunch.

6. Use a comma to set off introductory clauses.
   Though he started out as the nicest teacher in school, Mr. Post turned out to be a grouch.

7. Use a comma before the state in an address.
   Chicago, Illinois

8. Use a comma between the day of the month and the year.
   January 30, 1950

9. Use a comma to separate degrees and titles from names.
   Amanda R. Tyler, Ph.D.
   Thomas Johnson, Jr.

10. Use a comma to set off transitional expressions such as however, moreover, nevertheless, therefore, etc.
   I can't meet you today. I will, however, meet you tomorrow.

THE COLON (:)
1. Use a colon to introduce a famous quotation.
   I finally understand Thoreau's famous statement: "If a man does not keep pace with his companions, perhaps it is because he hears a different drummer. Let him step to the music which he hears, however measured or far away."

2. Use a colon to prepare the reader for a list or a series.

The recipe calls for: sugar, butter, eggs, flour, and vanilla.

3. Use a colon to follow the salutation in a business letter.

Dear Sirs:

THE SEMICOLON (;)

1. Use a semicolon to separate two independent clauses when the conjunction has been omitted.

The beach was crowded; we left quite early.

2. Use a semicolon to separate items in a series that contains commas.

The names on the mailboxes read: Gordon Black, Jr.; Chris Gaynor, M.D.; and Rich Rodgers, D.C.

QUOTATION MARKS ("   ")

1. Use quotation marks to indicate titles of poems, essays, short stories, songs, and articles.

Did you read Poe's "The Tell-Tale Heart"?
My favorite song is "Send in the Clowns."

2. Use quotation marks to enclose a person's direct comments.

"I had a wonderful time," shouted Bess.

3. Use single quotation marks to indicate a quotation within a quotation.

"Yesterday," Connie said, "the baby said 'Mama' for the first time."

THE EXCLAMATION POINT (!)

1. Use an exclamation point for special emphasis, or to indicate emotion.

Watch out!   Help!   Stop it, now!

PARENTHESES ( )

1. Use parentheses to set off material not grammatically related to the rest of the sentence. The material should, however, explain more about the sentence in which it appears.

If you buy that dress (and I hope you do), be sure to wear it to the dance.

NOTE: Any punctuation mark belonging to the phrase that appears before the parenthesis is placed *outside* the second parenthesis mark (see example above). Only when a separate sentence is placed in parentheses is the final punctuation mark placed *inside* the parentheses (see example below).

This exam is worth one-half your final grade. (That's why you should try to answer every question.) All papers must be turned in by three o'clock.

2. Matter enclosed in parentheses within a sentence (even if it forms a complete sentence by itself) need not begin with a capital letter and need not end with a period. But, if it is a question or exclamation, it must end with the appropriate mark.

When I bought my car (it's an old, used one), suddenly I had a hundred new friends.
Lois told me that you're moving (are you?) and that she'll never see you again.

UNDERLINING (_____)

In writing longhand and in typing, one line under a word stands for *italics*.

1. Use underlining to indicate titles of novels, plays, paintings, newspapers, magazines, TV shows, and movies.

<u>People</u> magazine is full of gossip.

You must read George Orwell's <u>Animal Farm</u>.

Did you get today's <u>Daily Sun</u>?

The movie <u>Jaws</u> was very scary.

THE APOSTROPHE (')

1. Use the apostrophe to indicate possession. (Add an apostrophe and an "s" to most words to create the *singular* possessive.)

I held Nancy's cat.

2. Use the apostrophe to indicate possession of a *plural* word. (If it does not end in "s," add an apostrophe and an "s." If it does end in "s," just add an apostrophe.)

The dogs' food might spoil.
The children's teacher is brilliant.

3. Use an apostrophe to indicate the plural of numbers, letters, words, and symbols.

Tony got all A's.
How many 3's are in your address?

4. Use an apostrophe to show where letters have been omitted in a contraction.

Ruth doesn't like pizza.
I can't read your writing.

MANY HAPPY RETURNS: UNDERSTANDING YOUR TEACHER'S COMMENTS

When you get back a paper don't look only at the grade. If your teacher has made comments *read them over carefully* and use them to guide you in writing future papers. (It pays to hang on to old compositions at least for one semester or else to keep some sort of record of your strengths and weaknesses. This way you can watch your progress from assignment to assignment. For more on this, see page 114.) Only when you understand *why* you got the grade you did — whether an A, B, C, or lower — will you be able to learn how to either stay on top or rise to the top.

Frequently, because of the volume of papers they correct, many teachers use a type of shorthand or code to let you know what grammatical or mechanical errors you've made in your composition. What follows is a set of commonly accepted and useful symbols. (If your teacher uses any symbols that aren't listed here, jot down his or her originals in the blank spaces provided.) If you understand what these symbols really mean, you'll learn a lot more from your mistakes the next time around.

SYMBOL	EXPLANATION
awk	awkwardly expressed sentence or paragraph
cap	use a capital letter
frag	sentence fragment; incomplete sentence
gr	grammatical error
M? *or* nc	meaning is not clear
p	punctuation error
pron *or* ref	unclear pronoun reference; what does the word refer to?
rep	awkward repetition
r-o	run-on sentence
sp	error in spelling
t *or* vt	incorrect verb tense
ww	wrong word — choose a better one

_____	_____
_____	_____
_____	_____
_____	_____
_____	_____
_____	_____
_____	_____
_____	_____

Chapter 5

WRITER'S CHOICE: 105 IDEAS FOR EVERY KIND OF PAPER

During any school year, you will probably write a number of compositions. *Descriptive, narrative, expository*, and *persuasive* are terms which stand for the four main types of writing. Learning what each type consists of and how it can benefit your particular paper will add style and variety to every assignment you do — from single paragraphs to twenty-page term papers.

Although each type of writing will be discussed separately in this chapter, keep in mind

95

that they frequently work together within a single composition. Description is very much a part of both narration and exposition; narrative writing is used at times to highlight expository and persuasive themes; and expository writing is often included in persuasive articles.

Following the explanation of each writing type are ideas that can be used to create a paper in that style. And, the last two sections of the chapter are devoted to two types of expository writing assignments dear to the hearts of every student — the essay test and the book report. After reading some A+ tips about these two feared (and sometimes hated!) compositions, perhaps you'll relax a bit more when the next one rolls around.

PICTURE THIS: DESCRIPTIVE WRITING

If you've got an eye for detail, descriptive writing should be a breeze. Writing a descriptive composition demands that a person look closely at the world and react to it intellectually and emotionally. The most necessary skill for this type of writing is the ability to use *all five senses* (sight, hearing, smell, taste, and touch) to observe and record your surroundings precisely. In a descriptive paper your aim is to create a picture of your subject in the mind of the reader. Naturally, the sharper and clearer this written picture is, the better the reader will be able to visualize exactly what you mean.

96

Some techniques that you can use to increase your reader's awareness and make your writing more descriptive are:

1. realistic details
2. specific, concrete language
3. vivid similes and metaphors

(For more on how to brush up on these techniques, see "Tell It Like It Is," in Chapter 3, page 60.)

The more observant you train yourself to be, the better word pictures you can "paint" for your readers. So, grab your "brushes" — here are some ideas for that next descriptive writing assignment:

Describe . . .
1. the first thing you saw when you woke up this morning
2. a fire
3. a stranger who walked past you today
4. love
5. a favorite meal
6. what it feels like to be bored or lonely
7. what happened fifteen minutes ago
8. your family's car (*or* truck, motorcycle, boat, van, etc.)
9. the qualities desirable in a good friend
10. having a tooth drilled and filled
11. yourself
12. the sights, sounds, smells, and tastes associated with your favorite holiday
13. strange noises in the middle of the night
14. a favorite movie or television star
15. your room as you left it this morning

WHAT'S THE STORY? NARRATIVE WRITING

Since everyone likes a good story, it's no wonder that the narrative is such a popular form of writing. Fairy tales, anecdotes, short stories, novels, plays, comics, and even some poems are all examples of the narrative form. Simply stated, a narrative is a story based on fact *or* fiction.

Any type of narrative (or story) writing is built on a series of events. By telling about these events one after the other, just as they occurred, your story will satisfy a reader's curiosity about what happens next. (A more complex narrative device of moving back and forth from past to present within a story is called the *flashback* technique.)

A narrative composition can be used to entertain, make a point, and/or illustrate a premise. Whatever the purpose, you may want to experiment with developing characters, setting, mood, and dialogue. (If you use dialogue remember the basic rules — 1. everything actually being said is enclosed in quotation marks and, 2. always begin a new paragraph whenever a new character begins to speak.) You'll probably find as you write your story that you will rely on description to add color and life to the events. This is only one of the many ways in which the different forms of writing interact with one another.

If you can tell a story, you can write a story — or narrative — composition. Here is a list of ideas to get you started:

1. Trace your family tree, then write a story about one of your long-lost relatives. It may be fact or fiction.

2. Select a famous historical incident or event and write an account of it as if you were a participant.

3. Write a story to accompany a famous photograph, painting, or drawing.

4. Write an updated version of a well-known folk or fairy tale.

5. Write a story that takes place fifty years from now.

6. People-watch for an afternoon. Then write a story based on someone you spotted.

7. Take notes first thing in the morning about one of your dreams. Expand your notes into a fictional story.

8. Write about a day in the "life" of an inanimate object. (Suggestions: a mirror, football, quarter, refrigerator, rug, or paperclip.)

9. Build a story around the popular proverb, "Better late than never" (or any other proverb of your choice).

10. Write a story (in prose or poetry) appropriate for a very young child.

11. Write a short story or play using the people in your English class as the only characters.

12. Write some funny dialogue between a father (or mother) and his/her daughter (or son) who must explain why she/he is two hours past curfew.

13. Give yourself a role in your favorite TV show. Then write the story of the episode you are in.

14. Rewrite a comic strip story in the style of a factual news story.

15. Take an anecdote from your experiences and write it up in comic-strip format.

FACTS OF THE MATTER: EXPOSITORY WRITING

The purpose of expository writing is to communicate factual information in essay form. It demands interest in and knowledge of a subject, *plus* the ability to organize these facts and opinions in a logical way. Once you practice the different kinds of expository writing, you'll find it to be the most practical and useful skill you can master.

In general, there are three particular types of expository essays: exposition that *defines*, exposition that *informs*, and exposition that *explains*. Although one composition will very often contain all three types, it's a good idea to get acquainted with each separately.

Expository essays that define call for short or extended definitions to help both the writer and reader understand the meaning of a word. Depending on the length of your essay, you may choose to develop your definition by *examples*, *comparisons*, and/or *functions*. Try any one of the following:

A hibachi is _____

Bad luck is _____

Gourmet food is _____

A digital watch is _____

A greeting card is _____

Pride is _____

Ballet is _____

A shoelace is _____

Warmth is _____

Delinquency is _____

Time is _____

A potato chip is _____

A clown is _____

Summertime is _____

Superman is _____

Expository essays that inform tell a reader "everything he always wanted to know about _____." Included are such things as essay test answers, book reports, outside research papers, and lab experiments. Their purpose is to inform others about something they might not be familiar with. (Unless, of course, your reader is your teacher and the occasion is a test. In this case, he or she will be on the lookout for specific information to be included.) Here are some suggestions for informative essays. If you're not familiar with the subject, do some quick research.

Equal Rights Amendment

Your best friend

Skylab

4-H Clubs

Chiropractic

The Olympic winners

Censorship

Nuclear power

A person you admire

Juvenile crime in your town

Your part-time job

The latest fad

Roller skating

Chemical preservatives

The athletic teams at your school

For more information on essay tests and book reports, see the special sections at the end of this chapter, pages 106–113.

Expository essays that explain tell "how-to" do something in such a way that anyone who is not acquainted with the process can understand it. Try explaining:

How to bathe a dog

How to balance a checkbook

How to train a parakeet

How to perform a magic trick

How to fall in love

How to eat spaghetti

How to tell time

How to break a bad habit

How to drive a car

How to play basketball

How to get to your house from school

How to change a light bulb

How to choose a ripe melon

How to lose gracefully

How to wallpaper a room

POWERS OF PERSUASION: PERSUASIVE WRITING

There's no doubt that your personal opinion enters into many of the papers that you write. But a persuasive composition is built on opinion. In it you use your own experiences, thoughts, and/or impressions to make a point, convince someone about an idea, or debate one side of an argument or issue.

You can write an A+ persuasive paper if: 1. you have a good case, 2. you are thoroughly convinced of something, and 3. you present your beliefs in a well-organized, sincere manner. Probably the most important thing to remember about persuasive writing is to choose your words carefully and be alert to their connotative and denotative meanings. (See "Shades of Meaning," Chapter 3, page 63.) You also want to make your argument believable and here are three suggestions on how to do just that:

1. Cite facts to support your point of view. (Name the sources of these facts if there's a chance your readers might question them.)

2. Relate a personal experience or incident if it is relevant to the topic and supports your point of view. (Don't, however, throw in a story just for laughs or to take up an extra 150 words. If the incident has nothing to do with the point of your essay, save it for cafeteria conversation.)

3. Quote authorities who support your viewpoint. (Your Aunt Roberta, unless she's a doctor, might not be a good person to quote on a medical issue.) Certainly you can quote someone you know, but make sure that that person qualifies as an authority and will help you to convince your readers.

Get ready to practice your powers of persuasion. Here are some ideas:

1. Write a magazine advertisement to sell one

of the following items: last year's calendar; one shoe; a safety pin; string; crab grass.

2. Write an intelligent plea to your parents asking them to extend your curfew by two hours.

3. You hate the latest fashion in clothing. Write an essay telling why.

4. Enter an imaginary contest. Win an imaginary trip to Italy! Write a letter convincing the judges that you really adore Thinetti Spaghetti Strands.

5. Convince someone — in writing — to buy your used car.

6. Tell why or why not cigarette smoking should be against the law.

7. Write a letter persuading someone to lend you some money.

8. Write an essay telling why _____ should be President of the United States.

9. Write a paper convincing people that you really saw a UFO.

10. Imagine that you're running for mayor of your hometown. Write a campaign speech convincing the people that, "You're the One!"

11. Write an article telling the public that they should never watch TV again.

12. You are falsely accused of cheating on the final exam. Write a note to your teacher convincing her/him that you were not cheating.

13. Write an article for or against the death penalty.

14. Write a review of a local restaurant, convincing everyone to eat there.

15. Write a review of a book, convincing everyone not to read it.

TEST PATTERNS: A+ ESSAY TEST TIPS

An essay test requires you to demonstrate how well you understand the ideas presented in class, rather than simply stating a memorized fact. Answers may range from one paragraph to many pages, with the majority falling into the "few paragraphs" category.

The A+ tips that follow are based on the assumption that you have studied the material you're about to be tested on and that you do understand it. Believe it or not, lack of preparation is not the biggest cause of poor grades on essay tests. A lot of F's owe "thanks" to misinterpretation of the question, poor organization, and unclear expression of ideas. It's time to tackle those problems right now!

Your performance on any essay test is directly related to how well you understand what is expected of you. As in any written assignment, you should not begin until you're quite clear about where you're going with the material. Usually the wording of the question can provide you with a clue about how to organize the answer. Following is a "crash course" on "clue words" often found in essay test questions. Learn what they mean and you'll save yourself a lot of time when the pressure is on.

ANALYZE — Take it apart and determine what makes it work.

CITE — Mention or quote.

COMMENT ON — Discuss, criticize, or explain.

COMPARE — Examine two things and tell their similarities and differences.

CONTRAST — Examine two things and tell their differences.

COMPARE AND CONTRAST — Tell the similarities and differences between two things. Same as COMPARE.

CRITICIZE — Give your judgment or opinion of something. Show its good and bad points.

DEFINE — To tell what a word or a phrase means. This often requires memorizing a definition.

DESCRIBE — Present a detailed account or word picture in a logical sequence or story.

DIAGRAM — Make a graph, chart, or drawing and label it.

DISCUSS — Talk about a subject by carefully presenting various points with supporting evidence. Cover the pros and cons.

ENUMERATE — Name, list, and number the main ideas one by one.

EVALUATE — Give your opinion (or an expert's opinion) of the value of a concept. Tell the advantages and disadvantages.

EXPLAIN — Give the *reasons for* or *causes of* something.

ILLUSTRATE — Explain or make clear by using concrete examples, comparisons, or analogies.

INTERPRET — Explain the meaning of something.

JUSTIFY — State why you think something is so. Then give reasons for your statement or conclusion.

OUTLINE — Give a general summary. List only the main ideas (and some supporting ideas). Omit minor details.

PROVE — Show by argument or logic that something is true.

REVIEW — Summarize important parts and criticize.

STATE — Describe the main points in brief, clear sentences.

SUMMARIZE — Give a brief account of the main ideas. Omit details and examples. Similar to OUTLINE.

Once you fully understand what you are to do, it's time to get organized. But before you write even one word on your test paper be sure to take into account the period of time you have to work. Get organized by planning a rough time schedule. (Unless you can complete all the questions, your grade might suffer.) If your teacher assigns different point values to the various questions, obviously, you should spend more time on the ones worth the most points. Most teachers won't object to your answering the questions out of order as long as they are correctly numbered on your answer sheets.

To save time and get a higher score, outline what you want to say in the essay. You can do this on scratch paper, in the margin of the test paper, or, if you have a good memory, in your head. This by no means has to be a formal outline, just a listing of all the facts, names, dates, and examples you want to include. Check them off as you develop them within the essay.

Organize your answer so that the first paragraph gets directly to the point. Let your teacher know from the very beginning that you know what you are talking about. The rest of your essay should support and develop the topic statement with facts and examples.

When you've adequately covered the main points, stop and move on. You don't need to write extra paragraphs to prove your knowledge of the subject. Your teacher usually has a definite idea of what she or he expects the answer to include and, the sooner its mentioned, the better.

ON THE BOOKS: CREATIVE BOOK REPORT IDEAS

Do you love to read but cringe at the thought of writing another why-I-did-or-did-not-like-the-book assignment? Do you find that you write down *everything* that happened in the book to prove to your teacher that you read it? Do you consider a good report one that simply paraphrases the back cover copy? Well, if you're bored writing a book report, chances are your teacher will be bored reading it.

The book report is a special kind of essay because of all the options open to you. Any book report can be made into a paper that defines, informs, explains, persuades, and/or describes. It is clearly an opportunity to be creative. Take advantage of it!

Following is a list of ideas for really challenging and imaginative ways to present your book report. Hopefully, these ideas will encourage you to analyze and constructively criticize what you read, and you'll learn more from a book than just the author's name. These kinds of reports can be so much fun to write that you might even look forward to your next assignment. Just check with your teacher before beginning the assignment in case she or he has some specific guidelines not mentioned in this book.

1. You are an interior decorator. Design a new home for the main character(s) in your book. Choose a style that you think would best suit your "client," for instance, futuristic, Danish Modern, Early American, or French Provincial. Describe your plans in detail or draw pictures of them.

2. Create a new character for your book. Explain what he/she could add to the story in terms of other characters, plot, etc. At what point would you introduce this new personality? Rewrite a short section of the book, introducing your new character into the story.

3. You've been hired to produce a film for the book you have just read. Which contemporary stars would you cast as the various characters in this novel? Why? Discuss the physical and personality characteristics that make each star the most desirable person for a particular role. (If

your novel has already been made into a film, ignore the original cast and choose your own.)

4. Discuss the importance of setting in your novel. Bring in photographs and/or make a slide presentation of the areas featured in the book. Did this particular setting add to or detract from the story? Was it an integral part of the plot? Imagine you could change the setting — where could you envision the story taking place? Why?

5. As an astrologer you are well-acquainted with the different personality traits associated with the different birth signs. Choose the sign that best fits each of the major characters in your novel. Give reasons for your choices. If the book is non-fiction, give reasons why the personalities do or do not fit their actual signs.

6. Pretend you are a psychiatrist who has had several sessions with a character from your novel. The character has left your office and you are jotting down your notes. Share some pages of your notes that analyze the conflicts and problems of this particular character.

7. You are planning a party with a theme based on your novel. Describe your ideas for invitations and decorations as well as food and entertainment. If you're really ambitious, you might create samples of the invitations or some decorations. Explain what the theme is and specifically which characters will be invited.

8. You are out at a Chinese restaurant with the main characters from your book. On this particular night the fortune cookies are amazingly appropriate. Describe each character and tell what his or her fortune cookie said and why it's fitting.

Don't forget to include yourself!

9. Working with another student who has read the same book, develop a "Meet the Author" spot for a talk show. (For ideas you might want to tune in to such television shows as *Today*, *Good Morning America, Tonight*, or any local radio interview program.) One of you should assume the identity of the host/interviewer and the other that of the author. Both of you should work together in advance of your scheduled "appearance" to develop good questions. Most questions should apply specifically to the book; some may relate, however, to the author's personal life (information from the book jacket or a biography about the author will help you with this part).

10. Pretend you are a judge reviewing the case presented in your novel. What would be *your* verdict?

11. Design a series of comic strips which illustrate several scenes or themes from your book. Reproduce dialogue from the book itself or create new, appropriate dialogue to fit the sequences.

12. Pretend you are one of the judges for the Pulitzer Prize for Literature, an annual award honoring excellence in writing. Decide whether or not you would nominate the book you've just read for such an award. Then write a letter to the author explaining why you've accepted or rejected his or her work to compete for such high honors.

13. You are fixed up on a blind date with one of the characters from your book. You are thrilled when you open the door! Tell who is standing there and explain why you are so happy. Now

imagine that you are miserable when you open the door and feel like slamming it in this person's face. Who is it? Explain why you are so disappointed.

14. Your job is to design an ad campaign to promote your book. Think of ideas for a new cover, inside jacket, poster, window banner, and display carton. Sketch your ideas or put them together to form a display. You might want to present your ideas in the form of a sixty-second TV or radio commercial.

15. Imagine that you are a talented, sought-after screenwriter hired to develop a television mini-series based on your book. Decide what parts you are going to adapt for the "small screen" and describe what you will include, exaggerate, or drop entirely. Write a draft of the first episode which must introduce the characters and basic plot and make people want to tune in again next week.

CHARTING A WINNING COURSE: A PROGRESS CHART FOR COMPOSITIONS

This chart is provided as a way for you to keep track of your progress in writing. After reading over each paper that is returned to you, make a note of your teacher's comments about your composition's strengths and weaknesses. In the last column at the right, write a short reminder of what you'd like to work on in your upcoming papers.

Glance over this chart at the start of each new assignment. By refreshing your memory about previous strengths and weaknesses, you are less likely to make the same mistakes twice. And, as the school year progresses, take pride in watching these weaknesses turn into strengths.

Composition Title	Date	Teacher's Comments	Areas to Improve in Next Composition

Composition Title	Date	Teacher's Comments	Areas to Improve in Next Composition

Composition Title	Date	Teacher's Comments	Areas to Improve in Next Composition

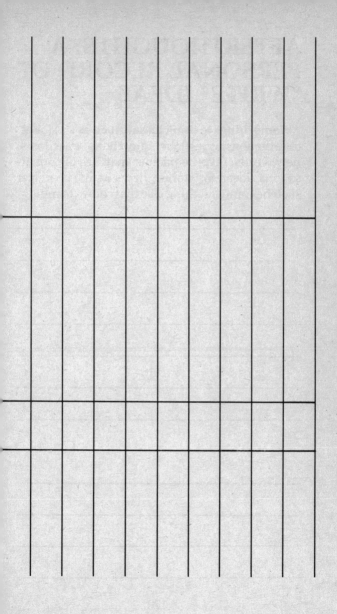

AFTERTHOUGHTS: A PERSONAL RECORD OF "WRITE" IDEAS

Some things to think about, such as . . . jokes, observations, questions, quotations, anecdotes, new words, favorite poems, snatches of conversations, ideas for stories, news items, character sketches, and anything else that comes to mind.

_____

_____

_____

_____

_____

_____

_____

_____

_____

_____

_____

INDEX